Best wishes and love
To you Channing.
We hope you enjoy
picking this up now
and then for new ideas

Grampuscat and Granny

GENERATION
to
GENERATION
Passing Along the Good Life to Your Children

by
TOM OWEN-TOWLE

Artwork by MILLARD SHEETS

SUNFLOWER INK
Palo Colorado Canyon
Carmel, Calif. 93923

Library of Congress Catalogue Card No. 86-061696
ISBN 0-931104-19-X

DEDICATION

This book is dedicated to two special kin:
CAROLYN and MILLARD

To CAROLYN—my beloved partner and co-parent.

As it has been said, the greatest gift a parent can give children is to love the other parent dearly and deeply...
and I do!

To MILLARD— my esteemed father-in-law, friend and collaborator.

I am inspired by your enormous talent and overflowing love...your love for beauty, life and family including three great-grandchildren, seventeen grandchildren and four children.

GENERATION TO GENERATION

In a house which becomes a home,
one hands down and another takes up
the heritage of mind and heart,
laughter and tears, musings and deeds.
Love, like a carefully loaded ship,
crosses the gulf between the generations.
Therefore, we do not neglect the ceremonies
of our passage: when we wed, when we die,
and when we are blessed with a child;
When we depart and when we return;
When we plant and when we harvest.
Let us bring up our children. It is not
the place of some official to hand to them
their heritage.
If others impart to our children our knowledge
and ideals, they will lose all of us that is
wordless and full of wonder.
Let us build memories in our children,
lest they allow treasures to be lost because
they have not been given the keys.
We live, not by things, but by the meanings
of things. It is needful to transmit the passwords
from generation to generation.

—Antoine de St. Exupéry

BEFORE IT'S TOO LATE

"There is a land of the living and a land of the dead. The bridge is love; the only truth, the only survival."

Thornton Wilder

Sometimes, we parents wait until it's too late to convey our love and pass on our beliefs to our children.

We wait until *we're* ready, but, by then, *they've* already flown the nest.

We wait for our children to seek our wisdom, but they seldom get around to it.

We wait for the right moment to open up and share, but it never seems to arrive.

We wait until our deathbed to tell them who we are and what we cherish, but it's too late.

Parenting tasks are awesome. Our tenure seems forever. But, sooner or later, we die. Parents suffer an unnecessary second-death, if we fail to transmit our values and visions to our children.

Failure to pass on ethical wisdom is a common familial plight. As a professional who does grief counseling, I am troubled by the amount of unfinished business at time of death, especially between parents and children.

Death is the final parting. It strikes us all, parent and child alike, one after another, sometimes in a strange order and often in anguishing, abrupt fashion. The tragedy of family death is compounded when it catches the household unprepared, when sentiments of love and principles of life have not been adequately shared.

This book is a guide for those parents who want to make peace with themselves and their children before it's too late. It is for those who desire "to transmit the passwords from generation to generation" while they are alive. It is for those who want to pass on to their children in clear, simple terms what "the good life" means to them.

I am one of those parents.

I recently decided to share love-letters with my children, boldly bequeathing some of my deepest concerns and hopes for them. I was ready and eager to make out what the Jewish culture calls an "ethical will".

When you are dying, you aren't always in the best condition to share your core. There is also little assurance that your family or friends will be in good enough shape to hear what you struggle to say.

Sometimes we are cogent during our closing days, but I wouldn't count on it. To compose our ethical wills amid low energy and high upset, low keenness and high confusion doesn't seem like a good time, and it usually isn't.

It's staggering how much effort, both logistical and emotional, we expend sorting out the distribution of our earthly goods. Many of us agonize over the passing on of our material possessions before we die. Which of the children should get our shell or stamp collections? Who would enjoy the dresser, the piano, the china?

Rationally, we parents know that once we give over our goods, it is up to our children to do with them as they choose, not as we dictate. Emotionally, it is difficult to relinquish precious possessions when we aren't certain how they will be treated. Will our prized goods be treasured or ignored, appreciated or stored, enjoyed or sold?

The sadness is that we spend an inordinate amount of energy and worry over our legal wills and so little effort on our ethical ones. What our children need more than our goods are our goals, more than our perishables are our principles, more than our possessions are our confessions and professions...in order to move ahead meaningfully with their own lives when we're gone.

I think of all the things Carolyn and I were going to write or say to our loved ones, but somehow never got around to sharing. Perhaps you do, too. We ministers are a lucky breed, because we get to preach what we practice. We write about and to our children all along the way, letting them peek in on some of our primary fears and hopes. But none of us parents can do this often enough.

I'm quite conscious of the intentional or unintentional burdens, pressures and guilts we adults can impose upon our children, all in the name of loving advice. As we depart our earthly abode, our temptation is to get in our last licks, which is all the more reason to shape our ethical wills when we are far from the grave.

In short, it appears wise to put a "disclaimer" at the outset of our ethical wills which might run something like this:

"*Loved Ones,*

These urgings of mine are to be filtered through your own hearts and minds and adapted accordingly. They are not commandments but reminders.

Neither bury them nor be buried by them. Listen to them as long as you can, and if you finish listening before I finish writing, put them away for a later reading.

Oh, by the way, I left wide margins for your own thoughts as you take in some of mine. I invite you to reach back as I reach out!

Yours,

Dad"

Why did I choose to write letters to my children rather than use another mode of communication? There are many reasons.

Letters are our most intimate form of written exchange. They enable us to be anecdotal and personal. I certainly don't wish to leave my children mere sermons or a reading list. A letter is just right.

Letters are a readable length. Who wants to wade through ponderous ethical essays? My desire is to awaken my children rather than put them to sleep.

Letters are a familiar form of human interaction. All ages know how to write them. Everyone enjoys receiving them, witnessed by our daily raids on the mailbox.

Letters are lifeblood to a love-relationship. My hope in this book is that Chris, Jenny, Russ and Erin will feel excitement when my love-letters arrive. Perhaps after reading them they will be sufficiently moved to write letters to their own offspring someday, to keep the chain going. But anything beyond their reading these letters is bonus indeed.

Moreover, letters are tangible, durable products

which, if carefully preserved, will last across the generations. Our children have long since forgotten many of our verbal admonitions or aspirations for them. Anecdotes, left to memory, are often mangled in the retelling.

On the other hand, letters, even some of our mediocre ones, tend to be saved by family members. They give our children something concrete to refer back to as they mature.

If your ethical will, or set of letters, is placed into an attractive, sturdy binder, I bet it will be preserved far into your children's futures.

I think of the aptness of Tillie Olsen's line: "Every woman who writes is a survivor." When we write, men or women, we are moving outside ourselves. When we write, we are risking our minds. When we write, we are publicly witnessing to what we hold dear. When we write, we reach within, reach out and reach beyond, venturing gifts in trust and love.

Through our letters we survive.

In summary, I don't want to go to the grave with my children guessing about my deepest wishes and challenges for them. An ethical will brings me closer to them during my life and after my death.

Why *fifty-two* letters? I wanted our children to read one letter per week. Each letter can be read in a matter of minutes. However, my hope has been that it may take a week's worth of reflection to digest them. Then a lifetime for each child to try them on for size.

MY LETTERS

"The only thing that we can leave behind us for persons to come is not systems, but confessions and professions. We can set them forth and say: 'This was my purpose, this was my wish, this was my thought...'"

Goethe

2

I LUCKY TO BE HERE!

"In a Pogo episode Churchy LaFemme sits wailing in the back of the rowboat after seeing a newspaper headline: 'Sun Will Burn Out in Three Billion Years Killing All Life!' Churchy cries, 'Woe is me, I am too young to die.' Porky reprimands him. He says, 'Shut up, you're lucky to be here in the first place!'"

Clarke Wells

Dear Lucky Ones,
You know what? The mathematical odds of your being born are incredible—something like one in 700 trillion. No two snowflakes are alike; no two humans are the same either. Even identical twins differ. Kids, it is a marvel

that each of you, irrepeatables, walks the earth at this moment in time.

None of us asks to be born. There is no personal merit involved with our arrivals. We creatures didn't earn the privilege of life. We were lucky. Whether you look at human existence scientifically or religiously, it is an unspeakable miracle, a wonder, a gift of grace.

My dear children, never, never forget that you have been loved into existence by your parents but moreover by a power beyond human creation, comprehension or control. I don't care whether or not you give a name to that power.

The important thing is to recognize that you didn't get yourselves here.

Let me tell you about a habit of mine upon rising every morning. I get up, take a deep breath and shout forth: "Hey, it's good to be alive. I'm downright lucky to be here. Thank you. Let's get started!"

That's not quite accurate. I don't always spring out of bed upon waking. I sometimes crawl or stumble out, but, always, thankful for life.

Another lucky one,

Dad

II WHY WERE YOU NOT ZUSYA?

"Before his death, Rabbi Zusya said: 'In the coming world, they will not ask me: 'Why were you not Moses?' They will ask me: 'Why were you not Zusya?'"

Martin Buber

Dear Unique Kids,

One of your main goals while on earth is to become who you really are. You are not Florence Nightengale or Michael Jackson, Jane Fonda or Moses. You are Chris, Jenny, Russ and Erin. Kids, please don't waste time being anybody else but yourselves. That will be enough challenge to consume your time and effort.

There is an Ashleigh Brilliant cartoon which reads: "I may not be totally perfect, but parts of me are excellent." I contend that each of you has many excellent parts to your being, more than you might even recognize thus far on your journey. Different parts in each of you, but excellent ones for sure.

One of you four children, I don't remember which one, came home one day from the primary grades and announced: "I think I'll finally try to be myself. I've tried everything else, and it

7

just hasn't worked out!"

Beautiful! Your learning was right on target.

Now, don't worry about deadlines in this search for self. You will need most of your lifetime to sort out just who you actually are. There is no rush. Move at your own pace.

Let me pass on to you guys one of my own discoveries. At age forty, no less. My finding had to do with my middle name "Allan".

"Allan" means "harmony" in Celtic and "hound" in Anglo-Saxon. A good, fitting name for one, who, like myself, is a Libra, that is, balanced and a bridge-builder.

I didn't know it as a child, but Allan is a name which matches up with my personality and profession. For I am a hound, always on the move, chasing down my visions, in hot pursuit of harmony and community wherever I go.

Aware and accepting of the discordant notes in life, I, Thomas ALLAN Owen-Towle, am most fully myself as a bridge, a binder, a hound after harmony, a believer that we humans can make a tuneful melody together. That's my goal. That's my name.

What does your name say to you? Seek out your special identity. Then salute it, nourish it, fulfill it!

I recommend that you take a personal pledge now rather than waiting until you are forty or retired. I heard the following vow, I think from a popular modern singer:

> *"So I hereby take myself, my soul doth take my heart, to honor, love and cherish till death do us part. . .what I have joined together, let no one put asunder."*

Children, consider taking such a pledge too. It may end up being the most important vow you make.

Love,

Allan

III   BE GOOD OR ELSE...!

"Be not simply good; be good for something."

Henry David Thoreau

Dear Chris, Jenny, Russ and Erin,
Remember when you were younger, your mother and I would make some remark to you as we left the house like: "Be good, while we're gone" or if we really wanted obedience from you characters, we would exclaim: "You'd better be good or else..."

We hoped by this off-hand threat that you would stay in the house and out of the street, out of the cookie cupboards, and most of all, out of trouble.

Now, in *your* teenage years and beyond, *we* have matured a lot. We have grown up along with you. We can now tell you that "being good" means much more than being tidy, sweet and staying indoors. It's even more than being nice and civilized.

Being good has to do with something deeper, broader and higher than neatness and safety. You see, kids, we didn't tell you the full story. We didn't let you know that the good person isn't always safe and often doesn't stay out of

10

trouble.

In a world that is cynical, the good person finds things to be cheerful about. In a world that is ugly, the good person creates something beautiful. In a world that can be downright mean, the good person tries to be a kindly soul. In a world of conformity, the good person is willing to take risks.

You live in a generation where lots of people believe, or at least they announce, that it doesn't pay to be good. They say that you might get hurt, lose your job, look foolish if you try to be good. Well, they're right! Sometimes good people stick out their necks and get clipped.

But I am inviting you children to stick out your necks for goodness rather than hiding them in shells. I am asking you to be good for goodness' sake, for no other reason than that in being good, you contribute to the joy and meaning of life.

I am inviting you to be good because that's why we are here on earth. In response to the undeserved gift of being alive, you and I are asked to make the only kind of repayment worth our humanity, namely, to be good persons.

Our earth will endure if enough people like you kids dare to be good from start to finish. Otherwise, we are in real trouble as a planet.

My friend, Glenn Brown (you may remember him), who was killed years ago in a tractor accident on his Illinois farm, used to tell me: "Tom, I spell God with two O's!" Children, you will learn that religious and political experts write fancy treatises and construct elaborate systems in order to make goodness sound real complicated and remote.

Don't be fooled! When the dust finally clears in your lives, if your highest principle, your view of God is spelled with two O's, you won't be far from the purpose of your being born.

A good person may be hard to be but is seldom hard to recognize. You will know when you meet one and when you are one.

Be good, be good...or else, or else our world won't make it and the lights will go out and all will be lost, for you, your children, and their children's children.

From someone else trying to be good,

Father

IV   TWO STATUES

"Freedom and responsibility are like Siamese twins—they die if they are parted."

Lillian Smith

My Dear Free and Responsible Children,

There is a story I once heard about a young girl who went to see the Statue of Liberty. It was such a powerful encounter that she was unable to sleep for several nights. Her mother, sensing discomfort, asked her what was the problem.

The girl replied: "I'm worried about the large lady with the lamp. She must get terribly tired. Don't you think that some of us ought to help her hold up that huge torch?"

Your job, my beloveds, in today's world is to help hold up torches like the torch of freedom, the torch of justice, the torch of peace wherever you might live.

In 1830, when William Ellery Channing (fifty years old at the time) was told by an acquaintance, "You seem to me to be the only young man I know," he replied, "Always young for liberty, I trust!"

You children may not now believe

13

it, but you will age. Instead of trying to reverse inevitable physical processes, I invite you to remain young for liberty, for justice, for peace, for love, for all that brings life.

I urge you to do your share in helping the large lady with the lamp!

We have a Statue of Liberty on the East Coast. None of you kids have seen it in person, but you may someday. Your lives have been lived in the Midwest and California.

To go along with the Statue of Liberty on the East Coast, don't you think we should have a Statue of Responsibility out here on the West Coast? Maybe we could locate it in San Francisco, San Diego or Los Angeles, smog permitting.

Others have also suggested this balance. For freedom without responsiblity leads to chaos. Responsibility without freedom hardens into obligation.

Liberty and responsibility belong together.

Here's to Two Statues!

Dad

V PLODDERS, INC.

*"And let us not grow weary in well-doing,
for in due season we shall reap, if we do
not lose heart."*

Galatians 6:9

Dear Plodders,

In our land where people want
results now and instant gratification is
almost expected, I must tell you that
lasting growth belongs to the plodders
among us. The swift may grow in spurts
but wear down over the long haul.

The plodders, though tired of
body and mind, keep running, keep the
faith, wait and receive second winds.
Sometimes life is a matter of holding on.
As the line goes: "The giant oak is just an
acorn that held its ground."

I want you to be numbered among
the plodders, perseverers and patient
rather than the quick, flashy and
impulsive.

I read where Thomas Edison, after
586 experimental failures to find the right
filament for the light bulb, had an
assistant who thought he would say
something appropriate. "It's a shame," he
said, "to have tried 586 times and failed."
Quick as a wink, Edison replied, "We
haven't had 586 failures." "But sir", the

assistant said, "we have."

"No," said Edison, "we now know 586 things that won't work and won't have to be tried again." He refused to be defeated. The rest is history. He was a plodder.

All important endeavors— partnership, parenting, vocation and social justice—require tenacity. So I challenge you children to get in shape now, to start plodding this very day.

I'll never forget the wisdom of one of your playmates down the block when you were quite young. Her mother asked this little girl what she learned on her first day of kindergarten. "Not enough," your friend answered, "not enough...I've got to go back tomorrow!"

So it is with all of us. We haven't learned enough, we haven't grown enough, we've got to keep on exploring this wonder called life.

We need to go back tomorrow for yet more purpose, more power, more experience!

Keep on keeping on,

Dad

VI   REAL STRENGTH

*"Nothing is so strong as gentleness.
Nothing is so gentle as real strength."*

St. Francis de Sales

Dear Children of Gentleness,
It is a rough and tumble world as
you have already noticed. In fact, it can
be mean and nasty. In such a world, I
invite you to consider gentleness.
Such advice may sound crazy, but
I give it anyway. Why? Because I remain
convinced that gently is the best way to
conduct our days. I'll go further; our
earth will survive only if gentleness
prevails in our interior, interpersonal and
international lives. Period.
When I was growing up, we boys
were taught to be gentle-men. For the
most part, this meant showing civil
manners. Then etiquette fell out of favor
in our land. I'm glad being well-mannered,
even mild-mannered, is making a
comeback today.
However, as an adult, I now
realize that being a gentle-man is a much
broader challenge than acting properly.
Gentleness is a lot tougher task than
opening doors, tipping hats and looking
spiffy.
No, at base, children, gentleness

17

has to do with real strength. We tend to think of gentle individuals as being soft-headed, pushovers, spineless. Not so!

The truly gentle woman or man can be as firm as anyone, but their firmness happens to be flexible and friendly. Gentle persons are as brave as they come, but they don't have to flaunt their courage or overpower anybody. They wear their moral muscle lightly.

Gentle people are willing to make up their minds and then change them if need be. They often back off so someone else might step forward.

I'm talking about gentleness from my own perspective. Listen to a similar reading from Adrienne Rich:

> "...gentleness is active
> gentleness swabs the crusted
> stump
>
> invents the more merciful
> instruments to touch the wound
> beyond the wound
>
> does not faint with disgust
>
> will not be driven off
>
> keeps bearing witness calmly
> against the predator, the parasite
>
> I am tired of faintheartedness..."

So, here you have it from a man and a woman that gentleness rather than control, arrogance or violence is the source of real strength in our lives.

Nature knows the power of gentleness as well. The tree which bends with the wind survives, and the water which yields to the rock in its path, eventually wears down the hard stone. Furthermore, as you kids know from our mountain hiking, the real climbers befriend rather than conquer mountains.

I'll never forget when we were climbing as a family once and one of you younger children was complaining: "It's not a path at all. It's all rocky and bumpy. I'll never make it!"

Our oldest child, Chris, responded in a brave and befriending fashion: "Sure, but the bumps are what you climb on!"

Children, I am confident that you will rarely go astray, if you practice the ways of gentleness, day in and day out, through fair and foul weather.

Gently,

Father

VII   BUILDING A CATHEDRAL

"Work is love made visible."

Kahlil Gibran

Dear Co-Workers,
I think you children have heard of Sigmund Freud by now. This great doctor of the mind thought our two most critical needs were "lieben und arbeiten", that is, "to love and to work". I agree.

If you are productive in your loving and your working, then you are likely to be happy individuals.

Chris, Jenny, Russ and Erin, I am

20

also convinced that there is available during your lifetimes, a job which will prove a good fit for each of you. Not a perfect fit perhaps, but a good one. A place where you will not merely be making a livelihood, important as that is, but also shaping a life.

You can't do everything. There are jobs you could do but shouldn't. Some will crush you; others you will botch. Nonetheless, I know there is a profession on this earth which you can profess with your heart, body and soul.

I believe you will be able to work your love and love your work during your stretch on our planet. So, go to it!

Three stonemasons were at work when a passerby stopped and asked of each one the simple question: "What are you doing?"

The first replied: "Obviously, I am cutting stone."

The second said: "My good person, I am earning a living."

The third lifted his eyes and said with a smile and with profound pride: "I am building a cathedral!"

My children, pursue your work with every ounce of excellence within you. Treat your post as a vision of great joy, beauty and worth as the third stonemason did. In so doing, your work will be honored and holy.

One final note. The longer I live, the more I realize that the good we do for ourselves often dies with us—the good we do for others and the earth lives on a long, long while, long after we're gone, long after we're even remembered.

Life is worth little unless it serves something greater than your own egos. Being a good carpenter, a good airline pilot, a good waitress, a good teacher is terribly important, but being a good professional isn't enough. Your profession must make the life of all whom you touch and treat richer, better, lovelier.

Being good, you see, at building a cathedral is necessary but insufficient labor. The cathedral must be good for something beyond itself.

I'm sure your cathedral will be. You've already laid some mighty impressive foundations.

Love,

Stonemason

VIII BEAUTY CROWDS ME

"Beauty crowds me till I die,
Beauty, have mercy on me.
But if I expire today,
Let it be in sight of thee."

Emily Dickinson

Dear Beauties,
    For all your blemishes and warts,
you kids have always been beautiful in
our eyes and will remain so. You can't do

anything ugly enough to wipe away your essential beauty. Therefore, you are beauties forever, as far as your mom and I are concerned.

But there are plenty of things you can do to enhance your beauty and that of the world in which you live. In this letter, I pass on a few notes on how you might beautify existence.

First, listen to what Emily Dickinson says in her poem above. Yes, beauty not only surrounds you, it enters, even crowds you. It pushes and tugs away at your lives every day. It is up to you kids to turn around and meet it, salute it, join forces with it.

May every day find you observing and making some beauty. And when the day expires, let it be in the sight of beauty. It isn't a luxury; beauty is a necessity.

A friend of mine once said: "Let me experience some beauty each day so that if I should die suddenly, it would have been enough!"

A second piece of wisdom about beauty is contained in Plato's *The Phaedrus* where it states: "May the outward and inward person be at one."

Some people work hard at being physically attractive and forget all about spiritual appearance. Others labor on their interior and neglect the exterior.

24

Children, don't fall into that either-or trap: both your inner and outer beings are worth beautifying.

Finally, don't just passively admire the beauty around you. Through the work of your hands and caring of your hearts, be beauty-makers so that when your days are complete you may join with the Navajo Indians in their ceremonial chant known as "The Night Way":

> *"Happy may I walk,*
> *In beauty, I walk!*
>
> *With beauty before me, I walk*
> *With beauty below me, I walk*
> *With beauty above me, I walk*
> *With beauty all around me, I walk.*
>
> *In beauty it is finished.*
> *In beauty it is finished.*
> *In beauty it is finished.*
> *In beauty it is finished."*

Amen,

Dad

IX   FIVE MINUTES LONGER

"Heroes and heroines are no braver than anyone else, but they are braver five minutes longer."

Ralph Waldo Emerson

My Fearful yet Brave Offspring,

I can't write a letter to you about courage without dealing with fear. They are connected.

Fear can be a signaling, prodding apparatus in our emotional lives. In the American classic, *Moby Dick*, the chief mate Starbuck says to his crew: "I will have no person in my boat who is not afraid of a whale." Melville goes on to say:

"By this, Starbuck seemed to mean...that an utterly fearless person is a far more dangerous comrade than a coward."

The point here is that courage, to be useful, dare not be blind or foolish. Remember that lesson, kids, and you will be saved a lot of unnecessary grief in your lives. You are already old enough to know the difference between bravery and stupidity. Right?

Fear cannot be banished from the human species, and if it could be, the

26

world might be more of a madhouse than it already is.

Fears, therefore, are not things to turn your back upon any more than they are things to drown in. I en-courage you to face your fears. Bravery is not the absence of fear; it is what you do with your fear.

Courage calms the mind. Courage allows time for wise decisions. It is that "five minutes longer" of which Emerson writes. We have tried to raise you so that you might be moved, at the right moment, to deeds of bravery.

Courage is primary. Without it we humans never leave the batter's box, we never get love or justice or forgiveness started. Without courage, we stay stuck.

With courage, you and I may be able to lick some honey off the thorns of life. At least, we'll try, won't we?

Your en-courager,

Dad

X   SEVEN AND EIGHT

"Such is life,
*   seven times down,*
*   eight times up!"*

Zenrin poem

Dear Comebackers,
This simple ten-syllable poem
offers wisdom.

Life is composed of comebacks.
The challenge for us is to emerge intact
from our scuffles and sorrows, our
frustrations and furies, to rise again from
the ashes of existence.

We need to get up one more time
than we have gone to the turf.

On every one of your birthdays,
your mom and I remind you of our
delight in your being alive. We also let
you know that your birth, as beautiful
and precious as it was, doesn't count for
much. The later, emotional and
intellectual, births matter greatly, for they
shape and refine your personhood.

Everyone is born, but not enough
people are reborn.

We need to be "created anew"
daily. We must believe, especially when
we are down, that we can get up.

No matter what we do, we can
take advantage of fresh chances. We can

turn around. We can start again. We are forgiven.

Sometimes you will be created anew, my dear ones, by your own intentional efforts. Sometimes it will be a gift from beyond your doing. In either case, renewal is available for your grasping. Rejoice in your renewability!

Mary Richards, the marvelous poet, potter and person writes:

> *"Perhaps if I had a coat of arms, this would be my motto: weep and begin again."*

You children have made numerous comebacks in your relatively short lives. You have come back from battered knees and bruised egos. I know. I have seen you rebound. Don't stop weeping and beginning again, all your days.

Seven and eight. Seven and eight. Seven and eight.

Your bruised companion,

Dad

XI THE MIDDLE PATH

"We always travel along precipices. Our truest obligation is to keep our balance."

Jose Ortega Y Gasset

Dear Jenny, Russ, Erin and Chris,
The ancient, wise religion of Buddhism has a lesson for you. It teaches the difficult art of maintaining balance. It instructs us to do this by pursuing the Middle Path between attractive extremes.

Following the Middle Path leads to understanding, which leads to peace, to the highest destiny of the human spirit. This process doesn't happen overnight. It takes a lifetime, kids, to grow skilled in the art of balancing.

Buddha was suggesting that we enjoy life and its many pleasures while not growing overly attached to any of them. When we repeatedly proclaim: "My stereo, my looks, my reputation, my future..." Buddha reminds us, young and old alike, that most human suffering results from clinging to such things, all of which are fleeting.

Buddha teaches that life is ever-changing, becoming. Therefore, we must learn to let things, people, experiences, life be. We possessive creatures need to

30

master the art of both sensitive holding and timely release, both aspiration and farewell.

We need to keep our balance in all our pursuits. You children know how easy it is to swerve this way or wobble that, whether driving or walking. It's also difficult to keep one's head while those around you are losing theirs.

It is a challenge to manage a wise Middle Path in your friendships, your jobs, your daily plans. Yet that is precisely what your mother and I urge you to do in growing up and on. We believe that balance remains a key to happy and healthy living.

Erin, when I think of you, I think of a fine, balanced young woman. Physically, whether tap-dancing or playing tennis you are poised and graceful. Emotionally, you keep your balance too. You are comfortable by yourself yet companionable with others. You can be serious *and* funny. You have an incredible imagination while living easily in the real world.

Let me give you another example of maintaining one's balance and perspective. The Nobel prize winner Linus Pauling was invited to a White House dinner-dance.

He spent the day picketing the White House in opposition to American nuclear policy. Then he changed to a dinner jacket and spent the evening as the late President Kennedy's guest.

Now, there was a person with a sense of proportion, a sense of balance, a sense of the Middle Path. He didn't waver. He wasn't without moral backbone. Each of his actions enhanced the other.

So, I welcome you children, one and all, to the balancing act called life. You will have many chances to walk tightropes every day.

It would bring me great pleasure to be a parent of four card-carrying members of the Middle Path club. They call us who have already joined: muddling middlers.

Welcome,

Dad

XII WHAT I GAVE, I HAVE

"What I kept, I lost.
What I spent, I had.
What I gave, I have."

Epitaph on an English gravestone

Dear Children,
As you well know, the art of
keeping isn't all bad. There will always be
secrets to keep, treasures to store,
memories to hold tightly. But some of us
keep compulsively; we keep, keep, keep.
We are hoarders. Although we keep
actual objects, we lose the joy of
possession.

To spend means to use up or pay
out. In either case, we expend, maybe
even exhaust, resources, if not ourselves.
However, at least in spending we no
longer withhold or hide something.

This epitaph closes by reminding
us that, when we leave life, we only have
what we gave and shared in love and
trust. You kids will find this one of life's
most difficult lessons to learn. Yet learn it
you must, if you want the full life.

All religions have promoted this
truth. I promote it again in this
love-letter.

When our lives come to the final
reckoning, we will realize that we are the

33

sum of our gifts—gifts of joy, gifts of time, gifts of dissent, gifts of comfort—all our gifts. We are not the sum of our possessions. We are not the sum of either our aspirations or accomplishments. We are finally the sum of our gifts.

Children, I have found this to be true thus far during my life. I also know it to be the case at times of death, when a person's character is weighed and summarized.

Let me offer a personal example of how I consider you and me to be the sum of our gifts.

My father, your grandfather, who is eighty now, still sells insurance for his livelihood. He has a client or two in San Diego and will drive down periodically from Los Angeles to take care of them.

He also visits us when he comes, taking us out to dinner and always, yes always, he brings a sackful of goodies for the family. All this activity is his way, one of his special ways, of giving to us, caring for us.

His care package contains things like roasted peanuts, toothpaste, soup, kleenex, razor blades, deodorants and toilet paper (just the right colors for the respective bathrooms).

He brings us these household items ostensibly because they were on

34

sale. He never fails to tell us that he got them at a bargain. I know better.

My father brings us toilet paper and the like, because he still wants to be recognized by his children as a caregiver. He has always been an extraordinarily generous person, and he's not about to stop being one coming down the homestretch.

You grandchildren are also the recipients of his generosity. He always brings you each a new Susan B. Anthony silver dollar for your savings. I think you would agree that there isn't a stingy bone in his body. In fact, all of your grandparents are giants of generosity.

Anyway, my father is reminding himself, as well as us, in these lavishings of love, that giving liberally of self and resources is finally what matters most.

His act tells us all that giving is humanity at its finest. He is showing us that we are truly the sum of our gifts.

Let's hear it for generosity,

Dad

XIII   PRACTICE DYING

Dear Russ, Jenny, Chris and Erin,
There is an old story that Plato,
on his death-bed, was asked by a friend if
he would sum up his great life's work,
The Dialogues, in one statement. Plato,
coming out of a daydream, looked at his
friend and said: "Practice dying!"
I think Plato's comment is
important. Let me try to make some
sense of it for you in this thirteenth letter.
First, picture two small children,
yourselves perhaps, talking to one
another under a tree. The one says: "It's
a beautiful tree isn't it?" "Yes, it is..."
"It's a shame that we won't be around to
see it when it's fully grown." "Why?
Where are we going?"
Young children don't envision
death. They understand sleep, even
separation, but not death, not the
cessation of physical existence.
Well, I want you children to know
that we adults haven't figured out death
either. Sometimes it seems as natural as
a tree losing its leaves. Other times death
is awful.
We rage at death because a
child's life is snuffed out prematurely.
Then again, we welcome it when a
person, at the end of a full life, dies

quietly in his or her sleep. It all depends.

Each death is different and singular just as each life is different and singular. Be careful not to consider all deaths as the same.

Second, it seems to me, kids, usually though not always, we die the way we live. If we live with a certain dignity and calm, that's often the way we conclude our lives. At least, that possibility is something to keep in mind as you carry out your existence.

Third, don't feel embarrassed if you believe in eternal life *or* if you believe that life ceases with death. You will be in good company with either belief.

I personally don't desire to live forever. The knowledge that I will die someday, and that's it, gives meaning to each moment of my life. When I know I won't always be around, I am motivated to plow more joy and love into every day I have. But, remember, that's merely my view; it may not be yours, now or ever.

Fourth, there will be times to either welcome or curse death when it comes. I hope you kids won't forget to laugh about it too. Here's a couple of Woody Allen jokes for starters:

> *"Death is one of the few things that can be done as easily lying down."*
>
> *or*

37

"I do not believe in an afterlife,
although I'm bringing a change of
underwear."

Finally, I want you to practice
dying. This means that every day of your
lives you need to be respectful of the
deaths going on in nature as well as the
shedding or dying transpiring in your
very own body. Did you know that your
entire body changes cells about every
seven or so years? A sobering thought,
isn't it?

If you are aware of the dyings
within life, if you allow yourself to die to
former possessions or ways of being,
then you children will be practicing the
art of dying.

You will be getting yourselves in
the best shape possible for the Big D
later on.

From one dying-and-living,

Dad

XIV YOUR VALENTINE!

"Being holy is majoring in love."

Dorothy Donnelly

Dear Lovers,

At some point, children, in your growing up, you have to declare your "major"—be it at the college level or later. You need to announce, primarily to yourselves but also to the world, your fundamental game-plan with the gifts and opportunities granted you.

I am partial, but I can think of no finer human major than love. I'm not

39

talking about a tiny or mushy love. I'm
not talking about a love which goes no
further than your own ego or emotions.
I'm talking about a love which reaches
within, reaches without and reaches
beyond. . . and then reaches some more.

I am talking about the kind of love
which the poet Marge Piercy describes
when she writes: "loving leaves stretch
marks". The real experience does just
that!

I invite your love to extend to the
impoverished, hospitalized, sick,
imprisoned, downtrodden and abused
members of the human clan. Your love
can never be too cozy or comfortable or
it isn't deserving of the name.

However, lest you become
lopsided lovers, remember to care deeply
about those persons right around you,
with whom you work and live: fellow
employees, family members, significant
others, brothers and sisters from whom
you may be alienated or parents who
need your forgiveness or friends who are
slipping away from you.

Loving cherishes and caresses
those both near and far. Every particle of
love is like another drop of rain on a
parched earth. I still carry in my wallet,
Chris, some words you wrote about love
when you were fourteen. Your statement
was beautiful then; it still is. It's the very

kind of love I am trying to describe in this letter:

> *"Love is a powerful meaning, and when that powerful meaning is used toward another person, it will raise that person eternally."*

Do you kids know the story of Valentine's Day? It is much more than a day of candy and romance. It has everything to do with both personal love and the broader concerns of compassion, friendship and justice.

Valentine was a Roman who was martyred on February 14, AD 270. He wrote a farewell note to the jailer's daughter who had befriended him while he was in prison, signing it, "Your Valentine".

At the close of our earthly stays, I can think of no more blessed way to sign the farewell note of our lives than with the phrase:

Your Valentine

XV WHERE ARE YOU GOALING?

"What good are strong and agile legs if we don't know in which direction to run?"

Michael Quoist

Dear Travelers,

By now you realize that there are plenty of people with sturdy bodies and sharp minds but who don't know where they are headed.

It is not enough to be a growing person. You need to discipline and direct your growth. Otherwise, like a rampaging vine, you can become unwieldy and out of control.

Many are the unsuccessful hunters who say that they did not aim at any particular part of the game they hunted, but at it generally. Even though you know I detest the thought of hunting animals, I think you get the point of the illustration.

You must make your goals specific, measurable and achievable. I encourage you children to aim particularly, and not generally, at work, at home, in both your private and public lives.

Think of yourselves as mice facing

42

a mountain of cheese. Your task is to nibble away at negotiable hunks of cheese until the whole thing is devoured.

We humans wear out or run away when we think of eating the entire mountain of cheese in a few sittings. We can't do that, but we can nibble away at it.

We can nibble away at our unhappiness. We can nibble away at a project. We can nibble away at improving our relationships. We can nibble away at saving the human race. We can nibble, nibble, nibble, day in and day out.

Remember a year is comprised of 365 days. We need to take one day at a time rather than nervously grabbing for a weekful of change and meaning. Moreover, each day is made up of twenty-four hours. Then there are the minutes, the smaller units.

Our task, as goalers, is to use well those smaller moments, the more manageable pieces of life, for each moment matters, each is sacred and to be treated as such.

I am recommending that you children take charge of your lives now, appropriate to your particular age. Go ahead, you can do it. Plus, you have our full blessing.

You and I, at different ages and stages, are like Gulliver. In his travels he ends up shipwrecked on an island, and while asleep, is strapped down by the Lilliputians with thousands of strings and pegs.

Instead of bemoaning these bindings, I say to you: consider breaking them, one by one, the real and imaginary ones, freeing yourselves to get on with your individual journeys.

Goaling,

Dad

XVI   *WE* ARE NUMBER ONE

"Let us be ashamed to die until we have won some victory for humanity."

Horace Mann

Dear Number Ones,
Kids fight all the time over being #1 in the eyes of their parents. You children have done your share of battling. So have countries. But lands go too far when the competitive drive is carried into international combat.

A cartoon depicts two people torn and tattered, absolutely alone and sheltered underneath heaps of destruction rubble. One person says to the other: "There's a rumor going around that we won!"

Dear children, World War III will be a war without winners. There will be no such thing as victory. It will only be a great collective act of suicide.

I believe that our toughest enemy is not Russia, and we aren't theirs. The real foe of us both is nuclear war. We must together find a nonviolent alternative to thermonuclear disaster. And rapidly.

That's why you see your mother and me working so feverishly in the peace movement. We are concerned for

45

you children, all children of the earth. We are laboring on your behalf. The torch will soon be passed on for you to be peacemakers.

As individuals, as teams, as nations we seem hell-bent on watching after and taking care of #1 who is none other than I, me, mine. It's odd, and unsettling, to reflect upon the fact that English is the only major language in which "I" is capitalized; in many languages "You" is capitalized and the "i" is in lower case.

If any of us would choose to be #1, let us be so in the things that really count, the things that make for a more beautiful life for humanity. Let us be #1 not only in technology but in ideals, not merely in material items but in principles and character.

I deeply believe, as a nation and a world today, we don't need any more big, blustery, brutal victories. We need victories for humanity not destruction, for love not power.

I encourage you children, as you assume your places in the adult world, to pursue victories over problems not peoples.

Did you know that the money required to provide adequate food, water, education, health and housing for everyone in the world has been estimated at roughly $20 billion a year? It is a huge sum of money...about as much as the world spends on arms every two weeks! Think about that.

We are #1, we are #1, we are #1. That's right, WE are #1. And the WE I'm referring to is the earth and all its people and other living things.

WE are #1. Let's keep it that way!

Dad

XVII   SELF-CARE

"Lara, at three, would circle the room, kissing each of us in turn. We welcomed our 'kissing fool'. Then she would kiss her own hand because, as she said, 'I love myself too'. My daughter, my teacher."

Greta Crosby

Dear Caregivers,

I'm sure there have been plenty of moments when we have come down too hard on you kids. We were anxious about your welfare, or we were blinded by our own expectations for you. In countless ways we have been unduly abrasive or harsh with you, the very ones we cherish so much.

However, if you children resemble the rest of humanity, you may be your own worst enemies. No one can be tougher on us than we ourselves. I bet you can think of situations where you have been uncaring, even mean, to yourselves.

Therefore, a big piece of my ethical will is to remind each of you to be good to yourselves. Be patient, be kind, be forgiving to yourselves. In short, take care of your beings from here on out.

There are many ways to show

self-care on a daily basis. Let me share some tips which have worked for me.

First, be quick and sure to praise yourself upon doing something as well as you could. Do this before you point out any blunders and flaws in your action.

Second, when you criticize yourself, make the criticisms constructive rather than destructive. Self-criticism should give you achievable options rather than unreachable goals.

Third, remember that the good life is a process not a destination. You are never grateful, generous and growing enough. But as long as you keep aspiring, as long as you stay on the road, you are moving ahead in the right direction. That's all you can ever expect of yourselves.

Fourth, simplify your daily routine as much as possible. Let those activities or ideas, aims or pressures go which no longer make sense to you.

Fifth, participate in at least as many cooperative events as competitive games. Pulling with others and not always pushing against them is a concrete way to care for your own being.

Sixth, find one endeavor each day where you are nice to your body. It requires considerable TLC. For some it's running, others swimming, still others working outside in the yard. Locate and regularly pursue the proper physical exercise for your body. It deserves daily care.

Do the same for your mind, your heart and your spirit. Your mind may need to be stretched by some reading or a discussion. For your heart do something encouraging, something that makes you feel proud of yourself.

We all need to feel heartened. A kind word or a thoughtful deed heartens me. I don't like to go to bed without having shared heartening moments each day.

Naturally, your spirit needs feeding too. Some form of meditation or reflection might work for you. Find time each day where you unclutter yourself and are still.

Finally, I would recommend that three or four times a year you write a "Dear Me" letter to yourself. In this letter remind yourself of all the things you enjoy about your special person and share ideas on how you can enrich that self.

I hope these self-care tips will help you along your way.

Caringly,

Dad

XVIII   THE YET FOLK

"In the midst of winter, I finally learned there was in me an invincible summer."

Albert Camus

Dear Erin, Chris, Russ and Jenny,
Tragedy is a universal experience.
You have had some in your young lives
already. So have your friends.

According to legend, when a
mother lost her child, Buddha said that
to be healed she needed only a mustard
seed from a household that had never
known sorrow.

The woman journeyed from home
to home over the world but never found
a family ignorant of some grief. In
learning that suffering was shared by all,
she was able to grow through her own
sorrow. She felt kinship. She felt support.
She was not alone.

There are many people who have
suffered greatly yet are able to endure, to
make it to the other side of the sadness.
There are people who rise triumphant
from the ashes of miserable childhoods.
There are people who overcome great
emotional liabilities or physical
handicaps.

You have met some of these folk
in your travels. Pay close attention to

them. They are true heroes and heroines. You can learn a great deal from them.

I call these people the *yet* folk. They are the humans among us who suffer cruelties *yet* still sing, who wrestle with pain *yet* soar spiritually, who face crisis after crisis *yet* continue to exude joy, who have every right to reek of resentment for their fate *yet* choose instead to live lives of happiness.

Yet persons demonstrate to the rest of us that resurrections are possible on days other than Easter.

I am very fond of the German poet Rainer Maria Rilke whose life, especially childhood, was filled with considerable upheaval and suffering. Among other discomforts and wrenchings, Rilke was bolted in the attic by his mother for blocks of time.

Yet he was committed to praising. He rose above his trauma to become a marvelous writer.

Children, think of those troubled ones you have known or read about who have been able to create an invincible summer in the midst of a terrible winter.

When you are beset by tragedy, be strong enough to join the *yet* folk. There will always be room for you there.

Yours,

Dad

XIX   CAPITALIZE THE HYPHEN

"You are my beloved, and you are my friend."

Song of Solomon

Dear Equals,
Your mother and I have tried to
live a marriage of equals as partners,
parents and professionals. We have
sometimes failed in this attempt, but we
persist nonetheless. It has been, perhaps,
our greatest contribution to your
upbringing.
Hopefully, some of our example,

however imperfect, will show up in the way you each choose to treat members of the opposite gender as associates, friends and intimates.

Before I go any further in this letter, let me share two common examples of what an equal relationship might mean. The first one will ring familiar from our country life in Iowa.

We like to think of our marriage as a team of horses. We must pull together, otherwise we can't farm. In a world of tractors, it may be tough to focus on farm horses, but you get the idea.

Second, imagine a rowboat. It has two oars. One person can pull on both oars at the same time, and the boat will move in the desired direction. But two persons can also sit side by side, with one pulling on the one oar and the other pulling on the other oar. As long as each individual pulls equally hard, the boat will move in a straight line; but if one is pulling harder than the other, the boat will go around in a circle.

Your mother and I have tried to row in a straight line all our married days.

There is another way of envisioning our marriage of equals. Have you heard of the concept of synergy? It means a "new thing is created without the loss of identity for the original elements that have combined together."

I visualize it best when I think in terms of 1 + 1 equaling not two but three. What your mother and I do together produces effects beyond what either of us could achieve alone. Joining our last names Owen and Towle in marriage expresses this conviction. Your mother once wisely commented: "We ought to capitalize the hyphen!"

Love between equals means that power is shared and mutual accountability is held for the quality of the relationship. It creates an enrichment, each person enlarging one's self through but not off or at the expense of the other.

But the issue is larger than one's marriage. I think we women and men in the world today need to care deeply about the welfare of one another, not more nor less than our own, but as much as our own.

With the presence of equality and empathy to break down the barriers of gender strife, friendship and love can follow.

There are two people hiking in the Vermont mountains and they run into a big, black bear. The one starts to change from boots to tennis shoes. The other says, "Hey, you won't be able to outrun the bear simply by changing your shoes."

The other replies, "I don't have to outrun the bear; I only have to outrun you!"

That's been the ongoing story between the sexes. For centuries men have been trying to overpower or outdistance women. Of late, women have been trying to run away or ahead of men.

It seems to me that gender strife, even gender racing, is an unwinnable proposition for humanity. Now, if ever, is the time to run alongside one another.

You know what, kids? We have the chance, for the first time in history, to become full-fledged friends as males and females. We really do, that is, if we have the courage to fuel our lives with equality and compassion.

We must choose to look one another lovingly in the eyes, to touch tenderly, and to say quietly: "From you I receive, to you I give, together we grow, from our shared gifts, we endure."

May it come to pass in your lifetimes,

A Believer-Worker

XX AMBIDEXTROUS

"To brave people, good and bad luck are like the right and left hands. They use both."

St. Catherine

Dear Agile Ones,
I urge you to learn how to be ambidextrous. I want you to be skillful enough to employ both your natural and minor hands in the flow of life.

I don't only mean this in a literal sense, but also figuratively. I simply want you to use all you have in greeting the whole of existence.

Here are some examples.

I asked myself the other day whether or not I would choose to have life void of any anguish. I realized that even if I were offered unadulterated bliss I would likely turn it down. I guess that's why the notion of "heaven" or "paradise" has never enthused me.

I'm saying, kids, that if you cut off despair, you cut off hope. Joy loses its edge without the presence of its partner, sorrow. If there were no clouds, we wouldn't appreciate the sun.

So it has been with my life. This is what I mean by using your left AND right hands.

Let me mention another example of ambidexterity. I want you to be good receivers and good givers as you advance in life.

Some people say it is more blessed to give than to receive, taking the cue from the biblical injunction. Others say, it is more blessed to receive than to give, taking their lead from the mood of our self-centered society.

I disagree with both extremes. I say: what is truly blessed is when we receive, to receive joyously, actively, thankfully *and* when we give, to give generously, exuberantly, lovingly.

There is a Jewish saying which reinforces this point: "The motto of life is: 'Give and Take'. Everyone must be both a giver and a receiver. Who is not is as a barren tree."

There are many other challenges of the ambidextrous life: be friendly yet firm, be patient yet ambitious, hasten slowly, and so on.

I've given you children a few paradoxes to practice for now. Can you think of any others? Good luck and much love.

As Always,

Dad

XXI THE ONLY EVIDENCE OF LIFE

Dear Children,
    I invite you to keep growing—intellectually, spiritually and emotionally—all your lives. As the poster in my office notes: "Growth is the only evidence of life."
    There will be times when you grow by leaps and bounds. Other times your growth will appear modest. The trick is to continue growing in one fashion or another right to the end.
    When we are young, our growth is evident. We grow like weeds. In the middle years, where I reside, one has to grow intentionally. You have to make a conscious effort to feed your soul and nourish your mind. If you aren't careful, they will get leftovers rather than adequate sustenance.
    Kids, having grown up, the challenge is to keep growing on.
    You will reach plateaus in your maturing, but your trip is not complete until you die and, even then, you close out your earthly existence somewhere in the midst of yet more pursuit and growth.
    Your path leads on. You never arrive. You will achieve significant

passages at twelve or twenty-one or
thirty or forty-seven or sixty-six or eighty-
nine or whenever along the way, but the
growing person treats those markers as
mere stations and continues forward on
his or her odyssey.

Let me tell you a story which I
heard from a friend of mine which
illustrates my point.

> *"When I was a boy, my dad took
> me on a trip through our garden.
> Dad was probably the best
> gardener in the community. He
> worked at it, loved it and was
> proud of it.*
>
> *After we finished the trip, Dad
> asked what I learned from the
> tour. The only thing I could see
> was that Dad had obviously done
> a lot of work in the garden. At
> this point Dad became somewhat
> impatient and said, 'Son, I had
> hoped you would observe that AS
> LONG AS THE VEGETABLES
> WERE GREEN, THEY WERE
> GROWING, BUT WHEN THEY
> GOT RIPE, THEY STARTED TO
> ROT.'"*

There are too many people in life
who get fat and ripe and then begin to

rot. I want you children to stay ever
green and growing, always open to yet
more wisdom and challenge in life.

Dad

XXII   NOBODY HERE BUT US CHICKENS

Dear Chickens,
I was recently reading a book of essays entitled: *Nobody Here But Us Chickens* by Marvin Mudrick. The title captures what I want to offer in this love-letter.

There are no angels around in life to carry us; only us chickens inhabit this globe. You kids have probably heard the story about four people named: EVERYBODY, SOMEBODY, ANYBODY AND NOBODY.

There was an important job to be done, and EVERYBODY was sure SOMEBODY would do it. ANYBODY could have done it, but NOBODY did it. SOMEBODY got angry about that because it was EVERYBODY'S job. EVERYBODY thought ANYBODY could do it, but NOBODY realized that EVERYBODY wouldn't do it. It ended up that EVERYBODY blamed SOMEBODY when NOBODY did what ANYBODY could have done.

So it goes in our person, social and global lives. But life is more a co-operative than a charity. You can not let Julia, George or even God carry the human race. You must play your special, significant role in the evolution of the universe.

I also think of the conversation between the priest and peasant while viewing the latter's fine garden. "You and the Lord," said the priest, "have worked well here." The peasant replied, "Yes, but you should have seen the place when the Lord had it all alone!"

You and I, with the help of the animals and the gods, are the tillers and tenders of this sacred ground called Earth. We are the *shapers* of political realities. We are the *sharers* of the time, talents and resources needed to keep our universe on course. Occasionally, we are even the *shakers* of foundations when things seem out of kilter.

Children, if you want a better society, it will be up to you to create one. If you want more education, it is your job to obtain it. If you want your partnership to deepen, then do it. If you want to be in finer physical, emotional or mental shape, then quit stalling and start working.

There are only us chickens around here.

One of them,

Dad

XXIII MIXED

"Could I ever be happy again now that I knew there was so much evil in the world?"

Selma Lagerlöf

Dear Kids,

If things were bad over 100 years ago, when Selma Lagerlöf lamented the state of her world, how much worse things are today after two World Wars and the threat of nuclear holocaust.

The modern world in which each of you children lives is filled with evil. The impulse to hurt and destroy property and persons has not been civilized out of us yet.

We humans are inclined to live well and live demonically. Sometimes on the same day.

There was the beggar who laid down in a barn and cried out, "How long, O God, am I going to suffer like this?" A voice from beyond responded, "Seven years." The beggar then asked, "And what's going to be, O God, after seven years?" The voice from beyond answered, "You'll get used to it!"

That's the first thing I have to say about evil. It is here to stay. You will simply have to get used to it. Evil lives on before, during and after we battle it.

Second, there is always a tremendous danger to fight evil as if it were something totally outside yourselves. I caution you to be wary of people who have no sensitivity to their own evil.

There is a Jim Crane cartoon which I plant on my desk to remind me of the temptation to ignore my own demons. It shows a person commenting upon the book which they are reading:

> *"I liked that monster story. It's the first thing in this book I really dig. Actually the world is filled with monsters. The good people don't have a chance. Lucky a few of us can still spot evil!"*

By the way, I share anecdotes and stories in my letters to you, because they make my ideas clearer and more striking. At least, I hope so.

Anyway, Victor Hugo wrote a story called "93". A ship is caught in a terrific storm, and when it is at its height, the frightened crew hear a loud crashing sound below. They know what it is.

A cannon they are carrying has broken loose and is crashing into the ship's sides with every smashing blow of the sea. Two people at the risk of their very lives manage to fasten it again, for they know that the heavy cannon on the

66

inside of their ship is a greater danger to them than is the storm outside.

So it is with persons and institutions. The burdens *within* can often be more destructive to all concerned than the storms *without*.

Third, I recommend a difficult thing. I want you to face your own evil tendencies squarely, even enter your own inner darkness as deeply as you are able.

"In Bimini, on the old Spanish Main," Loren Eiseley tells, "a black girl once said, 'Those as hunts treasures must go alone, at night, and when they find it, they have to leave a little of their blood behind them.'"

So it happens upon entering one's inner darkness. We are more frightened of our interior demons than most anything. We know their ugliness. We fantasize their tenacity. We are terrified to be alone with them.

Nonetheless, until you dare to greet and wrestle with some of your inner darkness, you will fail to uncover the full range, the real wealth of life.

This letter is a tough one, maybe unpleasant and scarey. But so is life. If what I'm writing bothers you too much or mystifies you, reach out to me, let's talk, I'm here.

In sum, we are mixes of good and

evil. Despite your mixture, there is no way for evil to block you from being happy humans. Evil will bug you, it should, but it need not overwhelm you as long as you are facing and fighting it all your days.

Your mixed-up Buddy,

Dad

XXIV   AN ANGEL IN THAT ROCK

My Creative Comrades,
There's the legend about the great artist Michelangelo pushing a huge piece of rock down a street. A curious neighbor, sitting lazily on the porch of her house, called to him and inquired why he labored so over an old piece of stone.

Michelangelo is reported to have answered, "Because there is an angel in that rock that wants to come out."

Kids, remember the angels you have shaped into being out of old pieces of rock. Think imaginatively. Think of rocks as those challenges which you have met. Think of rocks as those things you have tamed, or those times when you brought order out of chaos.

Whenever you find angels in rocks you are being creative. It is our creative potential that puts us in the image of God.

It is our charge in life to be creators. Some of you children will be creative with pen or brush, others with touch or thought. Be you a teacher or a veterinarian, a parent or a chef, an engineer or a musician you will fulfill your post through creativity.

Vincent Van Gogh used to say

that "many painters are afraid of the blank canvas, but the blank canvas is afraid of the passionate painter who is daring and who has broken that spell of 'You can not!'"

The creative individual doesn't run from the canvas or stare at it. The creative person paints.

Stay creative,

Dad

XXV ALONE...TOGETHER

*"We have all known the long loneliness,
and we have learned that the only solution
is to love and love comes with community."*

Dorothy Day

Dear Lonely Hearts,
I hope you children realize that
you will be lonely at times. You will
experience a lonely heart. That doesn't
mean you have to become permanent
members of the so-called "lonely hearts'
club".
We come into this universe alone.
We emerge from the womb naked,
yelping as we burst from a sheltered
solitude into an exposed, noisy scene.
We also exit alone, and even the
interlude between our birth and death—
whether painful, loving, boring or
happy—finds us ultimately alone.
As Samuel Butler reminds us all:
"Life is like playing a violin in public and
learning the instrument as one goes on."
Doesn't it make you nervous just
thinking about doing that? But learning
the violin, on stage, alone, is what life
asks us to do.
However, being alone or lonely
isn't the whole story, my dear ones.
We live alone...together. We

were also born, you see, through and into relationship. Plus we leave, or can leave, enduring influences upon other people when we die. Being alone yet together is one of the primary, persistent paradoxes of life.

My marriage, our family, my work and the larger community all remind me to commit my life, no holds barred, to being alone/together, in creative tension.

Every day may you have the courage to share both worlds, solitude and community, aloneness and togetherness, back and forth, from start to finish. You will be whole persons if you embrace them in rhythmic flow.

Another way to put it: when you look at your own navel, be reminded of both your uniqueness as an individual AND your vital connection to humanity.

Alongside,

Father

XXVI BE GROUNDED!

"Don't be humble. You're not that great."

Golda Meir

Dear Children,
Pride and humility when genuine are linked. Why? Because, as Meir rightly perceives, only those who have something about which to be proud, can properly be humble. When you have achieved something worthwhile, you feel confident about yourself. You don't need to be a braggart, simply proud.

Test it out. When you are strong and feeling good about yourselves, you can move comfortably alternating between feelings of pride and humility.

What about humility? What does it mean to be humble? Humility has received bad press lately. Society confuses it with humiliation or being humbled. Let me set the record straight about this unsung virtue.

Humility has nothing in common with self-effacement, martyrdom, putting yourself down. It is a lively quality which can lift you up and bring spark to your days.

You may know about the person who supposedly wrote a book entitled: *Humility and How I Achieved It!* Or, as another wit said, "Every time I think of how humble I am, I feel so proud!"

Kids, true humility, as you will learn, is a far cry from false modesty. It encourages us to act strongly but not overpoweringly. The humble person is confident but not cocky. They state their position but know well they might be mistaken.

Look deeper at the word "humility". It is "grounded", etymologically (there's a word for you to look up) and literally, in *humus*, the organic portion of our earthly soil.

Therefore, we humans, in being humble, are returning to our roots. We are earthlings, you and I. We come from the earth and will return to it. We aren't gods. We aren't devils. We are humans.

We are fallen creatures. We are going to keep falling from this or that flaw all our waking hours. The trick, kids, is to fall upward, or, more precisely, to fall forward. I believe that humility keeps us from toppling over altogether.

I heard it this way once. There are three kinds of people in the world. The kind who have their feet on the ground and their head in the sand; they are ostriches. There are also those with their head and feet in the clouds; they are the birds.

Finally, there are those with their feet on the ground and their head in the clouds. They are the balanced ones. They are the kind of humans of which we need more. They have wings and roots. They are grounded yet flying.

Be such!

Humbly yours,

Dad

XXVII   HOPERS

"Hope is the thing with feathers that perches in the soul, and sings the tune without the words, and never stops at all."

Dear Hopers,

You children will find that the toughest struggle going on in your lives, as well as in the world, is between cynicism and hope.

You will be sorely tempted to despair at times. I advise you: ward off cynicism and cultivate hopefulness. It is a choice you will be called upon to make daily.

The cynic says: "Blessed are they who believe in nothing, for they shall not be disappointed!" The hopeful person says, "Despite all of life's ills and problems, it is still a beautiful world!" Such an attitude, kids, will make all the difference in your world.

By hope I am not referring to optimism. The optimist tends to be a nonchalant, wishful thinker. The hoper is not assured that something will happen but is willing to work his or her head off that it might just come to be.

The hoper differs from the pessimist too. Realism would often

76

demand pessimism, but the hopeful one talks not in terms of crises but challenges. Crises can overwhelm and paralyze us. Challenges can be met.

I confess to being a hoper and want you to follow suit. I have a bias that no problem on earth is ever truly insoluble. Now, you and I may not solve it during our lifetimes. We may even commit omnicide as a race before any lasting answer arrives.

Nonetheless, I will do everything in my power to live a life which tries to solve problems rather than create them.

Hope is our sustaining friend. It keeps us going through the glorious days and restless nights of our souls. We *are* our aspirations and our dreams.

We live as we hope.

Dad

XXVIII GROW OLD ALONG WITH ME

*"The crucial task of age is balance...
keeping just well enough, just brave
enough...just honest enough to remain a
sentient human being."*

Florida Scott-Maxwell

Dear Growers,

"Grow old along with me" is a
phrase from one of Robert Browning's
poems. Like it or not, all four of you will
age. You will slow down and wrinkle.

The reminder in this poetic
fragment is for each of us to grow while
we are aging. Nothing you children do
will ultimately impede the withering
process, but everything you do can help
your growing.

As long as we must travel to
graves, I urge us to do so growing to the
last.

Most awake and vigorous people
age gracefully and remain fierce with life.
This is certainly the case with your
grandparents. You have been blessed to
be emotionally as well as geographically
close to your grandmothers and
grandfathers. All six of them.

They are examples of elders in
their seventies and above who have not
forfeited the spark of life. Their flames
burn brightly. Each in her or his own way

has kept growing not merely surviving. I hope that when you reach mid-life and head into your graying years, you will remember your grandparents with respect and fondness. Seeing them live life to the fullest reminds us coming after them that the closing years can be good, beautiful and expansive ones.

Your ancestors aren't the only folks full of fire to the finish. Read biographies of the most creative people in human history. Many of them never got going until late in life.

Grandma Moses and Colonel Sanders are merely two examples of people who found themselves as elders. Edith Hamilton also began her work as a mythographer after she retired from teaching at sixty. She inaugurated a series of four annual trips to Europe at the age of ninety.

To be sure, kids, there are people who start like gangbusters, then burn out, personally or professionally, in their thirties.

You can learn something from those who drop out or fade prematurely along the path, but you will learn the most from those who keep on growing to the end.

Grow old along with me,

Dad

XXIX   A RISING ON TOES

"Joy happens when a glow from within radiates outward. Joy is a rising on toes. There's no mistaking it. Joy is ecstasy."

Carolyn Owen-Towle

Dear Carriers of Joy,

Joy is not quite the same thing as delight or bliss. It is deeper. Joy is hard to explain, but your mother must have been referring to Jenny the jovial and Erin the exuberant when she wrote the above words. Clearly, once you experience joy, "there's no mistaking it."

Some reflections on this spiritual energy called JOY!

First, lots of people are happy and joyous when things are going their way. They bounce because life is bouncing.

The real challenge, children, is to bring and embody joy when those around you may be down or despairing. That's one mark of the truly joyous person.

Second, there needs to be some joy in all we do, even in our deeds of service and obligation. I like the way Mother Theresa put it: "First, I served the destitute out of duty, then out of joy, and finally I have come to realize that my duty and joy are inseparable."

I am talking about sharing joy in the

minor matters of life as well as during the major moments. Tucked away in a metropolitan newspaper was this brief comment on the death of an insignificant actor: "He played minor parts like a master." What more need we know about this person?

Our lives, children, are a mosaic of minor parts: dishwashing, mending clothes, writing notes, taking walks, answering doorbells, visiting the sick, breaking bread with friends, talking with loved ones, and performing a hundred commonplace tasks. How we play our roles in this daily drama called life truly determines the size of our joy!

Third, legend says, after death, the Egyptians were confronted by the god Osiris with a quiz that had to be answered honestly. After forty-two routine questions concerning how the deceased had lived, Osiris asked the main query which had two parts: "Did you find joy?" and "Did you bring joy?"

Those questions, dear ones, are crucial to answer. For everyone of us. Working or playing, dancing, thinking or even mourning, do we find joy, do we bring joy?

Joyfully,

Dad

XXX CONVERSE NOT CONVERT

*"Toleration is the greatest gift of the mind;
it requires the same effort of the brain that
it takes to balance oneself on a bicycle."*

Helen Keller

Dear Jenny, Erin, Chris and Russ,
The following letter has to do with
something more difficult than learning
how to ride your first bicycle.

Whether we name it toleration or
acceptance, the point of life is to be large
enough of spirit to listen to and learn
from another's viewpoint. We are on this
earth not to convert but to converse with
another. Many people never figure that
out.

I hope you children will spend

82

your days practicing the craft of conversation rather than conversion.

You have grown up in a religious tradition which has promoted tolerance and understanding from its start. Unitarianism rendered the first edict of Religious Freedom and Toleration in the Western World in 1568. You belong to this heritage.

I heard of two ministers who were always disagreeing on religious questions. Finally, one day they had been arguing some theological point more heatedly than usual.

Then one of them said, "That's alright. We'll just agree to disagree. The thing that counts is we're both doing the Lord's work—you in your way and I in HIS!"

Well, our religious claims are far less fixed than that. Instead, we say to each other: "You, my friend, are doing your work in your own way; and I in my own way. May we both be blessed and author wonderful creations."

I urge you children to defend the right of those who differ from you. More than that, I want you to hear them out.

Conversations strengthen our spirits and broaden our minds.

Dad

XXXI　DECIDUOUS

"It is only by risking our persons from one hour to another that we live at all."

William James

Dear Risk-takers,

Decision-making is difficult. We are fearful of making choices. The Latin word, *decido*, helps us here. It can mean "decide" or "fall off." Therefore, plants are deciduous if their leaves fall off in the winter.

Decidophobia is the fear of choosing, because we dread falling. Children and adults can suffer from this disease.

To choose our futures, we run the risk of falling or failing. It is no small matter to take our lives into our own hands and make conscious, considered judgments. When we allow outside circumstances or people to decide for us, we seldom, if ever, grow.

Children, I recommend that you be decision-makers rather than defaulters, active rather than passive individuals with the moments and projects facing you. Take risks.

Did you kids know that the word "heresy" comes to us from the Greek word meaning "choice"? Therefore, without personal choice you don't own much of anything in life. I invite you to be heretics, joining a fine and long tradition.

Sometimes you need the lead of a pioneer or a nudge from your heart to risk staking yourselves in new territory. If you can just manage a beginning move, the rest will follow.

John F. Kennedy, former President of our country, who was killed the year Jenny was born, loved the story told by Frank O'Connor, the Irish writer.

As a boy, O'Connor would make his way with friends across the countryside. When they came to an orchard wall that seemed too high and too doubtful to try and too difficult to permit their journey to continue, they took off their hats and tossed them over the wall. Then they had no choice but to follow them.

So it is with us!

Great decisions are never born; they are not made in heaven. They are lived. The real mettle of your character will be shown by how well you live with the choices you risk. Take off your hats and toss them over some walls.

A life without danger, without risk, without cost is a shallow one indeed.

Nudgingly,

Dad

XXXII KIN AND KIND

"If I cut a tree, my arm will bleed."

Alice Walker

Dear Tillers,
In the Garden of Eden story we
were told to tend it, "to till and keep it"
(Genesis 2:15), to be caretakers
alongside our sisters and brothers.

One of the meanings of the Eden
myth is that we receive existence
conditionally, and we must be obedient
to its basic laws. We were kicked out of
the Garden, and we are destroying it still,
because we refuse to accept life as
something deeded to us. We act as if we
own the earth.

Tilling means more than having a
green thumb. Some of us don't own
green thumbs, and we're not exempt
from the caretaking. You kids may
remember that I used to plant gardens in
our backyard in Iowa, a land with as lush,
fertile ground as exists anywhere on the
earth.

I learned always to keep the
empty seed packages. Sometimes they
were just the right size for storing my
crop! So, tilling and tending mean, green
thumbs or not, that we must all have
green spirits. We are charged to be

reliable stewards if not successful planters.

Let's face it, kids, if our earth is to survive, then you and your generation must proclaim that all life is interdependent and to be treated as such. We are of the soil, we are of the sea, we are of the air. Created of the same stuff, we are dependent upon one another. Dependent literally means that we all hang together.

No one is an island around here.

When will we learn that all forms of life are interdependent? The time, my beloveds, is now. The place to learn is here, on earth. Our very future banks on learning this lesson well.

The American Indians understood reverence for earth. They felt a unity with plants, rocks, animals and sun. We, who inherited this land from them, need to follow respectfully in their footsteps.

It is fascinating to me that the words *kin* and *kind* are related. If we realize that we are kin, one to another, we can't help but be kind to our sisters and brothers, soil and sky, animals and plants.

When I see the words kin and kind together, I think immediately of you, Jenny. I remember all the kittens you have rescued and brought home. You have always considered yourself a sister to the animals. Such a kind kin you have been to the life surrounding you.

Furthermore, all of you children have deep affection for and connection to the sun. As native Californians, you might even be considered sun-worshippers.

Anyway, members of the same common ancestry, cosmic clan if you will, we are going to survive only if we are humane and merciful partners with our earth.

The *uni*-verse is truly one. We didn't create it that way, but we can play a role in keeping it so.

Children, interdependence may turn out to be the chief insight and challenge of your lifetimes.

Live that way!

Dad

XXXIII   A FOUR-LETTER WORD

Dear Kids,

This love-letter may prove a sleeper.

There are plenty of four-letter words which are mighty important: good, play, work and love, among others. Being *lazy* is another one.

As you children grow (another four-letter word) up and on, I hope (yet another), you will learn to avoid the rat race.

You need to include moments in your existence when you just kick back, relax, unwind. It may be easy to do this now, but as you mature and assume more responsibilities, you will have to work at being lazy, if that makes any sense.

I personally have a problem with laziness. I often earn the right to be lazy but fail to exercise that right. I have needed to learn to balance my work with loafing.

So I share notes on the art of being lazy—notes which I'm swift to understand but slow to enflesh. Sharing them with you children reminds me to practice them.

Be willing to say *no*. Otherwise your yes-es will mean little. Say *no* to that extra duty at school or work which sends you into overload. Say *no* to an invitation to go out when you wish to stay home.

You don't have to explain yourself. You just want to be lazy.

When our yards are overgrown, we clean them out. Our agendas need pruning too.

The vibrant people I know are usually ones who know when and how to vary their schedules to include sufficient rest and plain old laziness.

Naturalist Louis Agassiz was once asked how he planned to spend his summer. "Crawling across the backyard on my stomach and observing insect life, blades of grass, the pebbles, and the earth," he replied.

"And what will you do with the rest of the summer?" his questioner continued.

"Why, it will take me the whole summer to get halfway across the yard," Agassiz exclaimed.

And so it should.

Lazily,

Dad

XXXIV   A HIGH AND HOLY DAY

"Power dwells with cheerfulness . . ."

Ralph Waldo Emerson

Dear Cheerfuls,

I think New Year's Day is one of the most important celebrations of the year.

It signals a fresh start. It means a second chance, a kind of reprieve, an opportunity for being better than before.

This holiday tells us that there are still options available, that it is possible to do something lovely and beautiful that we have never tried up to this time.

At New Year's Eve parties we make silly, nervous commotion because we are giving birth. We are about to

usher in something precious and new,
something both scarey and promising.

As you know, I strongly prefer
intergenerational New Year's Eve
gatherings over strictly adult ones. I push
for such events every year in our church.

I think it is crucial for children,
youth and adults, all of us, to stick close
at this moment of birth. I don't want
family and friends to miss out. I want us
all there—laughing, weeping, rejoicing
and welcoming.

In our frantic, zany New Year's
Eve frivolity we are saying with the poet
Browning, "Let us greet the unseen with
a cheer!" Kids, we don't know what the
future holds for us. We really can't
predict the happenings of our
tomorrows, our January 1sts and
beyond.

We are simply trying to greet the
unseen with a cheer. And why not? The
old year always deserves a cheer, and the
new one needs all the cheers we can give
it.

"Power dwells with cheerfulness."
Yes, it does!

Be of good cheer,

Dad

XXXV   SAVOR RATHER THAN SAVE

"Ultimately, time is all you have, and the idea isn't to save it but to savor it."

Ellen Goodman

Dear Children,

I suggest that you try not to save, steal or squelch time but to savor it.

I am tired of all the books and gadgets which urge us Americans to make short-cuts. We are fast becoming a society of microwave ovens and one-minute managers. Who are we fooling with all this one-minute craze?

My hunch is that those who so vigorously save time might need guidance on how to savor the time they save. Having more time, children, doesn't help one iota in knowing how to enjoy the extra moments. Some folks will always *fill* rather than *fulfill* time.

After all, good parenting, good loving, good times—most everything I call good in life—take a whole lot more effort than a matter of minutes. They take all I've got, indeed, a lifetime, to create and enjoy.

You and I have plenty of time, at whatever age, to do our deepest desires. We have enough time without having to slice, chop and cut up our days into a batch of "quickies".

We have all the time we need, if we but take it. As Tagore phrases it: "The butterfly counts not months but moments and has time enough." There's a good lesson for us humans.

Obsessive time-saving bothers me on another count. Why the rush? To what end? If it's going to take me one minute to be a good parent, then what's the point of parenting? I'm not involved in parenting for quickness or marriage to set a speed record. I'm in them for joy and nourishment, all my days.

One of the jokes around our household has been: "I'm sorry, I can't come out to play right now. I've got to stay in and help my Dad with MY homework!" Remember?

Yes, I was a stickler with you children about your homework each night. It often seemed to matter more to me than to you guys. I guess I wanted you to excel for my own ego too.

But I don't regret those daily dates with each of you. I can't imagine any better use of my time as a parent or person than to spend quality moments with my buddies. Soon enough, you characters would be off on your own, and I wouldn't have anyone with whom to do homework. Yours or mine!

As far as I'm concerned, they were irrepeatable occasions. I wanted to savor every morsel.

Our lives may be short, but never too short to do justice, love mercy and create good wherever we are planted.

Kids, I ask myself at various times during the course of each day: "What is the most important thing I can do at this extraordinary moment; for it will never be here again?"

Then I do it.

Savoringly,

Dad

95

XXXVI SEVENTY-TIMES-SEVEN

Dear Forgivers and Forgiven,

The scribes in the Bible taught that one should forgive three times. Peter was generous and suggested seven times. Jesus came along and said: "seventy-times-seven" (Matthew 18:22) which meant quit keeping score and stick to forgiving.

Forgiveness is a way of life. It must go on and on and on...as long as we roam this earth.

Kids, there will always be someone around to forgive or be forgiven by: your neighbor, an enemy, God, your parents, your co-workers, your partners, your children, your very selves.

The persons can be living or dead. Plus there are no time or geographical barriers to the act of forgiveness.

I'll never forget, Chris, when you asked us for forgiveness for something that had happened some ten or more years ago. We had forgotten about it. You remembered and needed release. This happens to all of us, as adults or children, at one time or another in our lives.

Forgiveness, naturally, isn't always easy or clear-cut to give or receive. We are often like the girl whose mother said,

"Now, Gertrude, your little brother is sorry he broke your doll, and I hope you will forgive him."

"Oh, alright, mom, but I will feel more like forgiving him after I slug him one first!"

A Chinese proverb is right on target when it says, "The one who pursues revenge should dig two graves."

Children, the fact is that hate never puts anyone in control. It does just the opposite. We are in bondage to our bitterness, our retaliation.

I can think of no finer example of forgiveness than the story of the Prodigal Son in the New Testament. The younger son seeks an early inheritance, goes off and squanders it in loose living. Then he sheepishly, even ashamedly, returns, asking for forgiveness, but expecting his just desserts.

Instead his father rushes out to greet him. Note the text says, "while he was yet at a distance", both emotionally and physically at a distance, the father embraced and kissed his son, rejoiced in his return and set the village to a mammoth celebration.

"Let us eat and make merry; for this my son was dead, and is alive again; he was lost, and is found." (Luke 15:24)

The son is accepted not because of any demonstrated worthiness, hardly, but is forgiven and accepted for who he is. Just accepted, no questions asked.

Forgiveness is not much in vogue nowadays, kids, whether between persons or nations. But, given the choices of avoidance, resentment or forgiveness, it is only the latter which brings us release and refreshment along the road.

Let's keep on forgiving,

Father

XXXVII THREE CHEERS FOR THE GRAY

"If I go to Heaven, I want to take reason with me."

Robert Ingersoll

Dear Reasoners,

I don't know much about heaven. Who does? But, children, I sure know the importance of using reason during our stay on earth. Don't travel the globe without it.

In an era of flamboyance, I applaud the relevance and limits of reason, perhaps the grayest of all the virtues.

Reason is a clarifying, steadying influence in a world which prizes the passionate and popular. Three cheers for the good old gray!

By reason, I mean guiding your beliefs and conduct by the evidence. I mean the will to make measured judgments. I mean the readiness to look before leaping, indeed, to look hard at all sides of an issue and to attach due weight to each side.

Reason is the *sorter* of our experiences. It enables us to wade through the trash of life without lugging it all into our living rooms.

Reason is also the *analyzer*. It sifts and weighs. It helps us order matters before any action.

Reason is a *formulator*. It organizes thoughts and feelings for purposes of understanding and expression.

Now, reason is far from a perfect instrument. It makes mistakes. But for all its flaws, the gray virtue serves us well.

Reason is our servant rather than our savior. It serves to help us obtain what we want. Think of reason as a forerunner.

Two of you children have participated in long distance running so you will be familiar with the concept of the "rabbit". The rabbit is a predesignated runner, in the field of entries, who takes off rapidly and sets a vigorous pace for the first half or so of, let's say, a mile race.

Then the rabbit drops back and allows the stronger runners to take over and make their homestretch bids for victory. The rabbit sets up and gives way. Without rabbits the results of the top milers in the world would be far less impressive.

Reason is a rabbit—a gray one at that.

Or to use another image: reason's work is not to play the instrument but to tune the strings. It readies us for bringing forth great melodies of delight.

Again I say, three cheers for the gray!

Dad

XXXVIII A CONTAGION

"As contagion of sickness makes sickness, contagion of trust can make trust."

Marianne Moore

Dear Children,
From your long and illustrious career as a newscarrier, Russ, I remember one of your early encounters with a customer. As this woman, nearly ninety, grew blind, she came to the place where she could no longer see to make accurate change for the paper when you collected.

One Saturday afternoon she drew her leather pocketbook with a snap on top from her purse, handed it to you and said, "Russ, I can't see very well any more; help yourself!"

102

As you opened the purse, you were suddenly struck with what a wonderful thing it is to be trusted.

Trust does not fool around with attempts at producing proofs. The fact is that you and I cannot conclusively prove to anyone, even loved ones, our trustworthiness. If we could, we would be talking about something other than trust.

To be inventing tests, to be suspicious, to check up all the time; these, children, are precisely what trust is not. At some point, you must take the leap of trust and place confidence in the character of lovers, friends, even acquaintances.

A woman carrying a heavy suitcase managed to catch a crowded streetcar. When she was safely aboard, the conductor noticed that she stood in the aisle clinging to her suitcase.

Finally, he said to her, "Lady, you can put your suitcase down now. The car will carry it for you." The same holds for trust. At some time, it nudges us to let go of whatever we are carrying. Trust asks us to trust.

Children, I believe that in matters of parenting and partnering, where trust is sorely tested, the depth and power of our love is in direct proportion to the supply of our trust. I think you kids would vouch for the fact that in our

103

family life when trust is missing, everything else goes downhill.

Trust is the foundation stone of our family structure.

The more we trust, the more trusting we become. It is contagious. The less trusting, for example, our country becomes of the Russians, the less trustworthy our behavior becomes toward them, and vice versa. Right now, neither land trusts the other much at all. Distrust keeps building, and the cycle just grows.

But trust can grow too! Our hearts, our friendships, our politics, our very lives yearn for trust.

I urge you to be contagious carriers of trust and trustworthiness, today, tomorrow, forever.

You will never regret it.

In trust,

Dad

XXXIX HISSING

*"A wild patience has taken me this far . . .
anger and tenderness: my selves . . ."*

Adrienne Rich

Dear Hissers,

Howard Thurman, the black liberal minister in his splendid meditative journal entitled, *Deep Is The Hunger,* relates the story in Buddhist writings concerning a village whose population was being destroyed by the periodic attacks of a cobra.

At length a holy person came to the village. The plight of the people was made known to her. She urged the snake to stop his destruction. The snake agreed to leave the villagers alone. After some time the people discovered that the snake was no longer dangerous.

Fear of the cobra disappeared and, instead, there developed a boldness, even meanness. The cobra's tail was pulled, water was thrown on him, little children threw sticks and bits of stone.

Finally, the snake's existence was increasingly perilous. He was nearly dead.

The holy one returned. The snake was livid. "I did as you commanded me; I stopped striking the villagers and now see what they have done to me. What must I do?"

The holy woman replied: "You did not obey me fully. It is true that I told you not to bite the people, but I did not tell you not to HISS at them!"

Call it healthy hissing or gracious grumbling. Call it what you will, we need it...in our partnerships, our families, our communities. The compassionate person may not strike but knows when to hiss: hiss sensitively and strategically.

Hissing is the same thing for me, kids, as showing my anger. Most confuse anger with hostility.

Anger is productive, if vented for impact. It becomes hostility, if released for injury.

Your mother and I try, upon going to bed, to work through our angry feelings from the day rather than harboring grudges or clinging to resentments. It may be good advice for you children too.

Hiss but do not bite!

Happy hissing,

Father

XL   STILL ASTONISHED

"You must not pity me because my sixtieth year finds me still astonished. To be astonished is one of the surest ways of not growing old too quickly."

Colette

Dear Wondering Ones,
Be wonderers all your days.
Wonder at things too beautiful for words.
Wonder at sorrows too piercing to be answered. Wonder at meadows, animals and flowers, birth and death and all the in-betweens.

We know enough to know that we know very little. We know enough, that is, to wonder, to feel curiosity about and marvel at life. Eddington, a physicist with a mystical bent, used to say, "Something unknown is doing we don't know what!"

The capacity to feel awe, to marvel, to be open to the miraculous in the everyday, to remain astonished when those around us are dreary and dragging. . .is a rare and special gift.

Children, if you have it now, don't give it up. If you lost it somewhere along the way, don't panic, you have plenty of time to retrieve it.

Open yourself to wonder.

Be wonder-ful.

To wonder is the greatest thing to which any of us earthlings can aspire. There is nothing above it.

Full of wonder,

Dad

XLI   SHARING A PECK OF SALT

"Wishing to be friends, as Aristotle wrote, is quick work, but friendship is a slowly ripening fruit. According to an ancient proverb which he quotes in his 'Ethics', you cannot know a person until you and they together have eaten a peck of salt."

Jane Howard

Dear Friends,

Parents and children, we already are. Moving toward friendship is our goal. I address you as friends in this letter, because that is one of the highest compliments I can ever offer you.

As you progress through the teen years and on into adulthood, our friendship is deepening. We aren't there by a long shot, but we are on the right path. As we all mature, we are opening up avenues for closer encounters.

We will never be peers, but we can be friends.

Did you know that the words "friend" and "free" grew out of each other? The Old English word *freo* meant free; not in bondage, noble, glad. The Old English word *freon* means to love, and the word *freond* becomes our modern English "friend".

You will learn, if you haven't

already, that true friends, while engaging in creative bonding, are people who leave you with your freedom intact.

Friendships cannot be forced or weasled, bought or pressured. They must be freely grown, on their own timetable.

Let me pass on a story.

When living in a different country and learning a foreign tongue, you often hear words or portions of words which sound just like your own language and, for a moment, you feel blessed with a piece of the familiar amid the strange.

Soon after my arrival in Germany, I heard a word pronounced, and spelled no less, just like an English word. The term was "gift"; and you know what it means in German? Poison!

Whenever I hear or use the word "gift" now, across my mind flashes a caution sign saying: "Beware—poison!" As if that vivid association were not enough to shake my awareness, I recently came upon four definitions of the word "gift" in Webster's New Collegiate Dictionary.

The last, but not least, of the definitions reads: "Obs. A bribe". The *definition* of gift may be obsolete, but the *reality* certainly is not. A good many gifts are still offered among us not as presents but as attempts to change or blackmail one another.

That brings me back to friendship.

Remember that befriending others must be a free sharing of gifts. It dare not resemble poison or a bribe or you will be in for a ton of grief.

A word about that peck of salt. A peck is a quarter of a bushel. That's an incredible amount of salt to share between friends, especially when many people today are on salt-free diets. But the point remains valid.

For friendships to flourish we must spend a lot of time together: wailing, celebrating, laughing, arguing, holding one another. I don't want you children to be misled into thinking that you can create friends in a matter of days. Genuine friendship is "a slowly ripening fruit". By the way, you don't need oodles of friends; a few good and loyal ones will do.

One final word about befriending. Samuel Johnson used the phrase "keeping one's friendship in repair". What a marvelous reminder.

Friendships aren't easy to establish. They take time, effort and freedom. They are even more difficult to sustain. They must be given regular check-ups.

You children will delude yourselves, if you feel you can maintain your companionships through sporadic feeding. No, friends are neither dispensable nor to be taken lightly. They require cultivation. They hunger for small yet regular displays of concern: calls, notes and remembrances of surprising sorts.

Then, when they are injured, they need repair, which is perhaps the toughest test of all.

Let's keep strengthening and nourishing our friendships as a family. It is one of our most cherished possibilities.

It lies at the heart of these letters.

In friendship,

Dad

XLII   TRUTHS

"Truth comes in small installments."

Clinton Lee Scott

Dear Children,

The main message of this particular letter is that there isn't one big Truth with a capital T, but many small ones which keep our lives motoring forward.

Some people strive to "find the whole truth, and nothing but the truth, so help me God"—preferably all at once. I find such folks a bit dangerous. They have been known to beat others over the head with what they've found.

I'm not sure we humans will ever know much about what might be called the final truth. That doesn't bother me. There are enough wisdoms and truths available to keep my life stretched and full. I hope you find this to be the case too.

I obtain pieces of wisdom here and there. A scientific truth here and

113

some political savvy there, some moral insight in the morning and some religious learning in the evening. These discoveries are sufficient to keep me hearty and well.

I have other words of caution about the business of truth and truths. Beware of people, including yourselves, parading around a half-truth as if it tells the total story. The rounded picture of life includes various angles.

The whole truth will always include something about both giving *and* receiving, ecstasy as well as agony. In our current culture there are those who would try to eliminate stress from our lives. That is a partial pursuit, a half-truth, for there are both eu-stress and di-stress in existence.

Furthermore, there are physical facts and emotional ones. You and your friend may agree on some external, objective principle of truth but sharply disagree on internal, subjective ones. Again, leave room in your mind for multiple truths.

Finally, there are three primary movements in truthing. First, you *seek* after truths; you are members of a continual search party, tracking down wisdoms in different regions of reality. Once you halt looking, you wither spiritually. You are called to be a person of the path.

114

Second, you will *find* truths. Some people live in a sea of relativism and chaos all their days, never admitting that they have discovered, at least, a few working insights for their lives. When you find a personal truth, shout for joy, embrace it, play, work and live with it. Maybe it will remain real for you for a long, long time. You will find that some of your current truths will last a lifetime. Others will not.

Third, you are charged to *do* truths. This biblical phrase gets to the heart of religious quest. Your lives, my children, will be judged finally not on how long you've searched or how many truths you've found but by how well you have lived the truths you've uncovered.

Be seekers, be finders, be doers of truths.

Faithfully,

Father

XLIII UNFINISHED ANIMALS

"Growth itself is the moral end. Not perfection, but the enduring process of perfecting, maturing, refining, is the aim of living."

Dear Unfinished Animals,
Children, we have been called rational animals, problem-solving animals, speaking animals. I like best the description of us as unfinished animals. I don't want you guys to get the brash notion that you have emotionally, intellectually or spiritually arrived during your stay on earth.

You are young now. You have reached a few of your dreams. Some have eluded your grasp. Just remember that you will close out your lives in mid-stream... having completed certain efforts, ignored others and still in the throes of others.

You are unfinished animals.

There is the story about a man who complained that he could never get caught up. Every day for twenty years he looked at his desk piled high with unfinished things, with papers, letters unanswered, bills to be paid, appointments accumulated, problems

116

that should have been settled two weeks ago.

When he walked out of the house to get away from the clutter, there was the grass that needed to be cut, hedges that should have been trimmed last spring. If he could only get caught up, just once, for twenty minutes in twenty years!

Then he slept and had a dream. He was in a large room with a beautiful mahogany desk before him, clean, bright and shiny. On it there were no letters or scraps of paper, no bills, no problems, no appointments—nothing.

Through the windows he could see the lawn and hedges neatly manicured, everything meticulously trimmed, in place. It was a great relief. He had caught up at last!

He was happy, at peace. Or was he?

All around the edges of his paradise there nibbled a little question: What do I do now? The mailcarrier came down the street whistling; he hailed him. He had no letters in his bag. He was just out for a walk. He had nothing to deliver. And the man asked: "What is this?"

"Why, don't you know?" said the postman cheerily, "This is Hell!"

All I know, kids, is that one of our primary qualities as humans is our

117

curiosity, our aspiration, our searching, our yearning, our meeting new challenges.

I want a desk with some tasks on it. I want mail. The alternative is hell.

I am happy to be an unfinished animal. I wouldn't want it any other way.

Love,

Father

XLIV GRATITUDE IS AN ATTITUDE

"I am grateful for what I am and have. My thanksgiving is perpetual."

Henry David Thoreau

Dear Thanksgivers,

Thoreau's thanksgiving was perpetual.

Most of us moderns specialize in periodic outbursts of gratitude. Rather than a continuous condition or a state of being, thanksgiving becomes an event, a time, a day, in particular, the fourth Thursday of every November.

I am writing this love-letter to you to persuade you that gratitude is an attitude, a perpetual one.

We Americans like to capture our hallowed virtues and cage them in measurable units of celebration. We have annual days honoring fathers and mothers and deluge our affection upon them during a twenty-four hour period. Commercial enterprises generate a staggering business out of our hectic, guilt-ridden eruptions of sentimentality.

Kids, when I was growing up, our society saluted inter-racial relations with what was then called "National Brotherhood Week". This was a valiant

119

but usually empty effort to effect reconciliation among the peoples of our neighborhoods.

I recall Tom Lehrer, the mathematician-musician, satirizing this program in one of his 1960's songs:

"During National Brotherhood Week,
Be nice to people who are inferior to you,
It's only for a week, so have no fear,
Be grateful that it doesn't last all year!"

You will learn that we humans not only wait to display our gratitude on scheduled times such as Thanksgiving Day, but also tend to do so only during triumphant moments. We are eager to declare thanks when things are going our way. A favorable outcome happens in our lives, and we are swift to be grateful. We are given a promotion at work, and we are filled with gratitude.

But thankfulness is not a matter of counting our blessings and curses at the end of the day and arriving at a verdict based on which side won. Gratitude remains a matter of spirit not statistics. It is an attitude.

Our culture is full of people who are grateful in spurts, when they are gratified, when they feel good. Actually, those who claim to be "more or less" grateful conduct lives of frustration and resentment.

120

People riddled with such mock gratitude are liable to make such biting comments as "Thanks a lot!" "Thanks a lot, Susan! "Thanks a lot, Mr. President!" "Thanks a lot, God!" Such remarks are bitter not grateful ones.

Kids, to keep myself in thankful condition, I do the following.

I launch my attitude of gratitude with the morning sun. I have found it renewing, upon rising out of bed, to utter in the silence of my heart: "I have completed safely another night of rest. I am starting a fresh day. I am thankful, I am thankful, I am thankful, and I will live this day as if I am thankful, from start to finish, come what may."

Whether you pray to the morning sun or bow to God, chant or dance, run or waddle in this morning ritual, it doesn't matter.

The crucial thing is to get yourself prepared for yet another day of thankfulness.

Crashes, victories and lulls will come and go. Our attitude of gratitude endures.

With thanksgiving,

Dad

XLV   SEXUAL ETHICS

Dear Russ, Jenny, Erin and Chris,

This won't be the first time we have talked together about sexual matters. Actually, we're not talking. I'm writing, and you're reading. So it's a different kind of situation. I've still got a few things to offer about this powerful area of our lives. So here goes.

You are sexual beings. You are ethical beings. One of my tasks as a parent is to help you grow a life where sexuality and ethics blend as beautifully as possible for yourselves and your partners.

I have learned, children, through positive and negative experiences over the years, that sex tends to run down and go sour when cut off from love.

I have found that what people, males and females alike, really want is to love and be loved. Embrace and be embraced. Cherish and be cherished. We want quality *and* equality in our moments of intimacy.

Relief from sexual tension is not enough, sexual variety is not enough, sexual ecstasy is not enough. Gratifying perhaps, but not satisfying enough over time. Bigger and better orgasms, nice and welcome as they can be, do not meet

122

the needs of our whole beings.

In an era of ugliness, we men and women yearn for some beauty. In a time of brokenness, we seek bonding. In a period of mistrust, we clamor for respect. We are desirous of length and depth to our sexual relationships.

There is a classic cartoon which has a young man saying to the rumpled and disarrayed girl he is passionately caressing, "Why speak of love at a time like this?"

We speak of love at a time like that because it's needed, it's appropriate, it's wanted, it's what makes the sexual experience truly worth it!

I've been speaking about having a *quality* sexual relationship as you mature. I would encourage you to seek *equality* in your partnerships too.

Sexuality is not something done *to* or even *for* another so much as *with* another. I urge you kids to pay full attention to the mutual needs and desires of whatever relationship you share.

Equal partners share the responsibility for their sex life, and don't blame or praise outside forces for the way their sexual love is going. They are in charge, equally so. I hope you four will remember that.

Children, if a relationship is controlling, undermining, lopsided

123

outside the sexual area, it will surely be no different inside the sexual domain. Our bodies can not practice what our minds are not affirming.

We are whole people. We are our sexuality. Let the whole of your lives touch and be touched. . .lovingly.

In the Song of Solomon we read that potent passage of partnered love: "You are my beloved, and you are my friend!" Sure, it's an ideal, but what's wrong with pursuing ideals, particularly in such a rich area as sexual love?

For partners who care, who are equally friends and beloveds, the sexual experience can be a varied yet continual renewal of our sense of unity. And such unity, such communion, is surely among the finest joys of being human.

In our best moments your mother and I are fortunate to share such joy.

We want the same for each of you.

Love,

Dad

XLVI   AWFUL ROWING TOWARD GOD

Dear Rowers,

For years now I have engaged in what Anne Sexton called the "awful rowing toward God".

My struggle with the divine is aweful because it is a venture full of awe and wonder. It is also awful, because it can be a frustrating, agonizing endeavor—this rowing toward God. It's a rowing, because it demands rigorous effort and

125

full employment of all the oars at one's disposal.

Finally, kids, I would say that my rowing is *toward* God. A few years ago I couldn't have said that. I was moving away from God more than toward God. I am now groping after, wrestling with and rowing toward divine presence. And it's awful most of the time.

My rowing is far from over. I don't expect it ever will be over. Sexton states in her poem:

> *"As the African says: this is my tale which I have told, if it be sweet, if it be not sweet, take somewhere else and let some return to me. This story ends with me still rowing."*

I bet my life will end with me still rowing too.

Kids, I have often preached about the nature of God as I perceive it. I hope you will someday take time to read my findings on this complicated religious theme.

Over the years I have talked about God as struggle, action, void, the ocean, good. At other times I have come up empty-handed in my searching for God. I have tried to be honest enough to report the missings as well as the discoveries.

The one thing I feel strongly about in rowing toward God is to share sufficient humor. A sturdy religion can afford humor. Henry Miller in *Tropic of Capricorn* wrote:

> *"I don't say that God is one grand laugh; I say that you've got to laugh hard before you can get anywhere near God."*

Be serious in your pursuit of God, but not too serious.

God likes a good laugh,

Dad

XLVII   CATCH YOUR BREATH

*"Do you want to get to death's door
without knowing yourself? Of course not.
Then take the time, enter your depths, get
to know your inner being!"*

Dorothy Donnelly

Dear Busy Ones,
You should never be too busy
that you avoid spending time with your
own self, your own "depths". A trip to
your interior castle (St. Theresa of Avila's
phrase) will renew and rest your mind
and heart during the tumult of your daily
life.

A minister friend of mine
meditates two and a half hours daily.
When listing the ten most important
things about herself, she mentions
"meditator" at the top. What inner
discipline and stamina! I can only "catch
my breath" in spurts.

Whether you children take up a
formal relaxation practice or not, I don't
want you to fail to try to befriend your
solitude, "to get to know your inner
being". Doing so may end up being one
of the most important treats you give
yourself daily.

I can't put this request too
strongly.

128

Your lives will get increasingly frantic and wild as you move further into adulthood. You will be avalanched with trivia and trauma. You will desperately need a place and practice where you catch your breath and rejuvenate your weary, worried, worn self. Believe me, you will!

One of the most common plights of our overstressed generation is that too many of us are always out of breath, winded, bushed.

I encourage you frisky characters to catch your breath. I ask you to be attentive to it, literally, to breathe slowly and deeply, letting go of every muscle and nerve, enjoying the experience completely, in short, unwinding, at least two or three times during the course of your day.

In rhythm with your breathing, you might consider thinking or even saying such phrases as: "I breathe in love and breathe out hate; I breathe in peace and breathe out stress!" Nothing fancy or elaborate, but it does the trick for me.

I pass on this breath-taking counsel to each of you.

Dad

XLVIII LAUGHERS LAST!

"There are three things that are real: God, human folly and laughter. The first two are beyond comprehension, so we must do what we can with the third."

Dear Laughers,

I love this piece of wisdom from the East.

Children, while God and human folly reside beyond our grasp, laughter abides in our very midst. We have only to open heart and mouth, and laughter rolls forth in ripples of release.

Laughter is one of our main tools to share what is bottled up inside of us: frustration, sadness and delight.

It cleanses our spirit, jiggles our body and refreshes our mind. You kids make sure that you have regular fits of laughter after breakfast, after lunch and after dinner, *and* as many other times as possible.

I have long believed that only when religion has honored both its serious and funny sides has it remained healthy and safe in human hands. If we can joke about what we cherish and love, then we have achieved freedom and fulfillment.

130

Laughter is physiological—certain muscles of the face contract and relax, and suddenly, sound explodes in the throat.

Laughter is psychological—being an expression of joy.

Laughter is also religious, for it is a saving grace when we are able to laugh at ourselves, as well as at life's funnies and flaws.

The great Danish theologian, Sören Kierkegaard went right to the heart of the religious venture when he wrote: "When I was young, I forgot to laugh. Later, when I opened my eyes and saw reality...I began to laugh and haven't stopped since."

That's certainly true for me. The older I get, the more there is to laugh about, the more time I take to laugh. In fact, in my summer diary of a few years back, I wrote the following:

> *"Perhaps, above all, I want to be remembered by my family as a caring fool, a serious yet zany person who really knew how to laugh with others, make them roar into a state of joy."*

I feel there is so much untapped fun and playfulness and laughter left in me. I just might keep on laughing, all the way into eternity.

Laughingly,

Dad

XLIX   NEVER RESTING IN PEACE

"Peace is possible only if we commit ourselves passionately to insist, resist and persist."

Katherine Lindsley Camp

Dear Children,

We need to *insist* that peace with justice be considered a priority by our elected officials. We need to *resist* when an individual is wrong or a system evil. We need to *persist* all the way. Such moral drive keeps us sane in a terrifying world.

Being a peacemaker is not merely a strategy but a way of life, to be embodied internally, interpersonally and internationally, for the long haul, or whatever haul our universe has. As May Sarton says: "So the peacemaker must...live with a long patience not to yield."

There is a character in one of Alan Paton's South African novels who said of going to heaven, "When I go up there, which is my intention, the Big Judge will say to me, 'Where are your wounds?' And if I say I haven't any, God will say, 'Was there nothing to fight for?' I couldn't face that question."

Neither could I. As your father, I

133

hope uneasiness before that question fills your souls too, so that you will be moved to insist, resist and persist in the name of peacefulness.

I read where activist Daniel Berrigan, when asked: "What would you like your tombstone to say?" replied: "May I never rest in peace!" That is the fitting response for those of us who would struggle all our days and nights for justice, mercy and peace on this earth.

Even in graves our examples will stir others to keep the faith and continue to be carriers of compassion.

I want there to be enough calm in your lives to bring you serenity, but not so much as to cauterize your moral nerve.

I recommend that your lives be filled with both peace *and* unrest.

Now and forevermore,

Dad

L MORE AND MORE MYSTERIOUS

"As you grow older, you only realize how many secrets there must be. Your sense of wonder increases. The more one penetrates the realm of knowledge, the more puzzling everything becomes. I find life more and more mysterious."

Henry Miller

Dear Children of Mystery,
You were born in mystery, live in the midst of it and will return to it.
Even if future generations solve problem after problem, ethical and political ones as well as personal ones, there will be mysteries left over, things

135

we humans can neither understand nor unravel.

My religion pushes my mind as far as it can go and then invites me to bow before the mysteries of evil and suffering, of life and death, of love and solitude, of god. I have found, kids, that most everything that has touched my life in a profound way has abundant mystery in it.

Don't try to scrub the world clean of its mystery. Don't reduce life to the logical and literal. Don't throw away myth and symbol. Don't ignore what you cannot comprehend.

Alan Watts relates the following story when talking about the power of mystery:

> *"Making sense out of the seeming chaos of experience reminds me of my childish desire to send someone a parcel of water in the mail.*
>
> *The recipient unties the string, releasing the deluge in her lap. But the game would never work, since it is irritatingly impossible to wrap and tie a pound of water in a paper package.*
>
> *There are kinds of paper which won't disintegrate when wet, but the trouble is to get the water*

*itself into any manageable shape,
and to tie the string without
bursting the bundle."*

Kids, life cannot be tied into neat
packages. It overflows with mystery,
always has, always will.

Your job is to plunge into the
mysteries. Open yourselves to their
perplexity and promise. Engage life, meet
death, surrender to love, wrestle with
evil.

Blessed are those who rather than
avoiding or explaining mystery have the
courage to encounter it, from beginning
to end.

May you be among the blessed,

Dad

LI   YES!

Dear Yea-Sayers,

A monk asked Joshu, one of the greatest Zen masters in China, "What is the one ultimate word of truth?" Instead of giving him any specific answer he made a simple response saying, "Yes!"

There are moments, children, to say *no* in clear and unmistakable terms: to deny, to negate, to cancel, to wipe out. The basic attitude of your beings, however, needs to be affirmation, a rousing, unapologetic, life-long YES!

We live in a nay-saying generation. Whether at school, work or play, there is always someone around with a negative attitude. They find fault with new proposals without giving them serious attention. They act as if their current job is only "temporary", expecting the "perfect" post to be elsewhere. They are waiting for an "ideal" partnership, thereby saying *no* to their current one.

Nay-sayers make global statements such as: "Politicians are no good." "Nuclear war is inevitable." "My children are always in trouble." "I wish I went to a different school or lived in a different state." Nay-sayers are demoralizing company. They drag us down.

138

One of our family friends once said about your Grandfather Millard: "He does what the others of us only dare to dream about." That's true. Your Grandfather has been one who has followed his hopes through to fruition. He has been an adventurer, a doer, a full-fledged yea-sayer. He hasn't let problems stop him. He has said yes amid dissatisfactions, yes despite reservations. He hasn't only discussed bravery, he has been brave.

I invite you to follow in the footsteps of your Grandfather Millard.

By now you know only too well that you can't drive a car with the brakes on. The way to drive ahead is to put your foot on the gas pedal and steer. The same is true with life.

The most important word in any language is YES. But don't just say it, children. Be and live lives of YES from now until your final breath.

Yes,

Father

LII PASS IT ON!

"David, what your Uncle Asher means is that a parent's love isn't to be paid back; it can only be passed on!"

Herbert Tarr

Dear Chris, Jenny, Russ and Erin,
It is strangely true that we parents are happiest and most fulfilled not when you children try to pay us back for anything but when you pass on any gifts we might have sent your way. Gifts of time, gifts of thought, gifts of meaning, any gifts which meant something to you, be they material or spiritual ones.

Teach someone else you love the card games our family enjoyed. Tell them the stories and jokes too. Sing with your own children the crazy old tunes you remember from our times together.

Pass on some of the peculiar traditions or habits our family grew around meals, holidays, trips. Yes, even be willing to drop those customs which you couldn't stand. We won't complain. We tossed out some of those from our parents too.

Few things continue uninterrupted forever. I heard of the little girl who said to her mother one day, "Did you once tell me that the blue vase in the front

140

room had been handed down from one generation of your family to another?"

Her mother replied, "Yes, dear, why do you ask?" The girl answered, "Because, Mommy, I'm very sorry, but this generation has dropped it!"

Tradition literally means that something has been placed in my hands and I, in turn, am urged to pass it on carefully. Of course, once someone has gifted me with a tradition, I have the right and responsibility to handle it in my own fashion.

I can let it be or modify it. Then, if I don't drop it, I pass it on. Finally, I stand back and permit others to do with it as they choose.

So it is with our lives as parents. We share things with you children, our most precious gifts, and then you handle them in your own ways. Each of you.

I only hope that there have been notions and nudgings in these fifty-two letters which might be passed on from you to your loved ones along your journey.

I have written you children trying to share pieces of my mind and heart.

Perhaps you will be moved to keep this tradition alive.

All my love,

Dad

P.S.—IT WORKS!

"There are only two bequests we can give our families, one of them is ROOTS, the other is WINGS. Families can help to provide both the security of roots and the inspiration of wings."

Henry Ward Beecher

You are probably wondering what happened when my children received their letters.

I have good news to report.

It works! The process and product work.

Our children welcomed them eagerly and read them enthusiastically. They felt proud, honored and blessed. The letters were gifts.

The only snag is that they want more letters. These fifty-two merely served as tantalizers.

So I'm back to work—taking more stock, making more notes and preparing more letters.

Who knows? I might be doing this the rest of my life: composing love-letters to my children.

That's fine with me. I find it a good use of my time and spirit.

You may be ready too. You may be ready to pass your version of "the good life" on to your kids.

Friend, I invite you to pass this book on to your kids, with personal notes, or write your own ethical will. . . before it's too late.

Doing this may turn out to be the most important achievement of your parenting career!

Mail Order Information:

For additional copies of *Generation to Generation* send $7.95 per book plus $1.50 for shipping and handling (ADD 6% Sales Tax—CA. Res.). Make checks payable to Tom Owen-Towle, 3303 Second Avenue, San Diego, California 92103. Telephone (619) 295-7067.

Also available through local bookstores that use R.R. Bowker Company BOOKS IN PRINT catalogue system. Order through publisher SUNFLOWER INK for bookstore discount.